SOLDIERS IN FUR AND FEATHERS

THE ANIMALS THAT SERVED IN WORLD WAR I – ALLIED FORCES

SUSAN BULANDA

Alpine
PUBLICATIONS
Crawford, CO

TABLE OF CONTENTS

CHAPTER 4 - THE PIGEONS   47

CHAPTER 5 - THE MASCOTS   59

LIST OF ILLUSTRATIONS

ACKNOWLEDGMENTS

Several people went above and beyond to help me with this book, and I wish to thank them. Nina Bondarenko, a canine behaviorist, scoured the books at the Cruft's Dog Show in England a number of years ago and found one of the rare books that I needed to research this work. I also thank Jack Keane, a former naval officer and an avid military enthusiast employed by Johns Hopkins Applied Physics Lab, for putting me in touch with Dwight Messimer, a World War I expert who was kind enough to review this manuscript and write the foreword for it. My thanks also to everyone at Alpine Publications for their work in making this book possible.

FOREWORD

Many of us have only a vague or general knowledge of how animals were used in wartime situations. Sue Bulanda has written an entertaining and interesting account describing how the Western Allies, particularly the British and French, used animals in what she calls a transition war, one in which animal-drawn equipment was giving way to machine-drawn equipment. This work is not just about the animals, however. Bulanda, who is a certified animal-behavior consultant and expert search-and-rescue dog trainer, has factored in the human–animal bond, something with which all pet lovers will identify.

For such a compact work as this one, she has provided a wealth of information ranging from the types of animals used, the reasons for their selection, and the wide variety of roles given to the animals. Understandably, war dogs get the greatest attention, and an entire chapter is devoted to mascots, most of which were also dogs.

Anyone who has ever owned a dog will thoroughly enjoy this book. After all, haven't we all owned exceptionally intelligent dogs like those featured here? Of course we have. And how many of us have bonded with our dogs to the point that they actually talked to us? All of us. So it was, and still is, with the soldier handlers who took, and will take, their dogs into battle. Obviously, their shared bond was and is unquestionably more personal and considerably more intense than many of us have experienced. After all, these war dogs protected soldiers' lives on a daily basis; their handlers were fully aware of how dependent they were on their dogs to keep them alive. When it comes to human–animal bonding, probably, the only experience that we fully share with soldier handlers is the excruciating pain we suffer when our pets die.

I am a military historian, and most of my research and writing have focused on World War I. However, other than basic rudimentary information concerning the roles of animals in war, I had little knowledge about the scope of usage practiced by the Western Allies in World War I, particularly the French. What little I did know was limited to the American Expeditionary Force. This handy book has been enormously helpful to me in filling that void.

For example, I did not know about a breed of donkey called a Poitou, which is considerably larger than the pint-size burro that many in Mexico and North America associate with the name "donkey." I knew that camels are obnoxious and difficult to deal with, but Bulanda adds details about these animals that I had never known. And I am sure that you will, like I was, be surprised at the physical punishment experienced by carrier pigeons, yet they managed to continue their flights to their destinations. I will keep this book on my shelf as one of the most useful and easy-to-access references on animals that served in World War I.

I will not take up your time telling you what is inside the book except to say that it is a very good read and will provide you with a host of interesting facts about the animals that were used at the front in World War I. The text is beautifully written, full of fascinating information, and well organized. So, get comfortable, settle in, and enjoy Sue Bulanda's, *Soldiers in Fur and Feathers*.

— Dwight R. Messimer, Mountain View, California, 2013

Dwight R. Messimer is a military historian who focuses on World War I, with emphasis on Germany's U-boat operations and on American POW escapes. He is the author of ten books on military and naval subjects covering both World War I and the early months of World War II. He has also contributed to several anthologies on military history and has written articles for Military History Quarterly and Naval Aviation News. He was an advisor on BBC's television series, "World War I," and appeared in History Channel programs on POW escapes. He is a retired college professor who lives with his wife in the San Francisco Bay area.

INTRODUCTION

While I was researching this book, I was able to purchase numerous photos and articles as well as a few rare books, some published during World War I and others shortly thereafter. As I studied these materials, what stood out—although sometimes not spoken about directly—was the deep affection and bond that developed between the soldiers and their animal helpers/companions. It did not matter what type of animal it was, the affection was the same. If you look closely at some of the photos, the pride and affection are evident in the soldiers' expressions.

Pet owners know how deep the bond with their pets can be. What we do not always understand is that when a person shares life and death experiences with an animal, or when the animal saves that individual's life—sometimes at the cost of the animal's life—the bond that develops is unique. It is difficult to put it into words.

I have had the honor of experiencing this bond with my search-and-rescue dogs during more than twenty years of field service. Military and police dog handlers—people who rely on service dogs—and other working dog handlers also develop this kind of attachment.

This bond may form from the intense training that a person goes through to qualify for a job or from the mutual dependence between that person and the animal. The individual becomes a working team with that animal. The relationship between pet owners and their animals is deep too, but it is different. I have been fortunate to experience both types of this human–animal bond, and I have worked with thousands of pet owners and with those who have working dogs. From these situations I have been able to discern the distinctions between these relationships, and they became even more evident to me as I researched the animals of the Great War.

The following poem was written by William H. Parr (in September 1919) and first appeared in *The Ladies Home Journal*. It was included in *Animal War Heroes* by Peter Shaw Baker (1933). There is no better way of expressing how someone feels about his exceptional animals.

His Two Horses
O Lord! To Thee I want to make my prayer;
    My soul is troubled sore from day to day.
I've never had the chance to know Thee, Lord—
    Nobody ever taught me how to pray.
So if my prayer is not as it should be,
    Is not as padre prays on church parade,
Please pardon me; forgive what I've forgot,
    For at Thy feet my naked soul is laid.

If in the roster kept by Thee above,
 My name is next to cease this life fatigue
And I must fall in with my fallen pals,
 A clean life's page behind I want to leave.
Grant that I die where bursting shrapnel sings,
 My team upon a gallop toward the foe,
And when my soul at last reports to Thee
 Please let me take my horses where I go.

If it is true what our old padre says,
 That there are horses in the land above,
Are there not some spare stalls to hold my two—
 My black, my brown, the horses that I love?
They're only common field-artillery plugs,
 As I am just a common soldier man;
We've fought and starved together side by side—
 I'd like to take them with me if I can.

I know my saddle black is pretty mean,
 And kicks and bites at everyone but me;
Still when I'm with him he is always good—
 Just let me bring him up for You to see,
He'd be ill-treated if I left him here,
 Be kicked and cursed and starved until he died;
Please, can't I ride him through the golden streets,
 The gentle old brown off-horse at his side?

They've carried me on many a weary ride,
 They've been my pals, my everlasting joy,
I've nursed them both when they were sick,
 And kept their harness burnished like a toy;
I've gone with them into the jaws of death,
 Gunners and drivers killed on every trip;
Their panting hides have dripped with mud and sweat—
 My horses needed neither spurs nor whip.

O Lord, if heaven has no stable room—
 With greatest reverence this I'd like to tell—
And if the fiery regions have some stalls,
 Then let me ride my horses down in hell!
And when the grand great, final roll-call comes,
 To be the first upon parade we'll try;
O Lord of all, please grant my only prayer—
 To take my horses with me when I die.

CHAPTER 1

BACKGROUND

CAUSES OF WORLD WAR I

World War I was also called the Great War because it was the first world-wide conflict. The events that led to World War I advanced rapidly and were somewhat difficult to follow because they were not as clear-cut as in subsequent wars.

According to historians, tensions were building up prior to World War I, but the spark that set it off was the assassination of the Archduke Franz Ferdinand, the heir to the Austro-Hungarian throne. Austria–Hungary blamed the "Black Hand," a Serbian nationalist secret society, for the assassination and therefore tried to control the Serbians.

A simple time line is as follows:

June 28, 1914—Archduke Franz Ferdinand is assassinated.

July 28, 1914—Austria–Hungary declares war on Serbia.

July 29, 1914—Russia, which has a treaty with Serbia, mobilizes its army.

August 1, 1914—Germany, which is allied with Austria–Hungry, declares war on Russia.

August 3, 1914—France, which is allied with Russia, is now at war with Germany.

August 4, 1914—German soldiers cross the Belgium border, a neutral country, so that they can reach Paris quickly.

August 4, 1914—Britain, which is allied with France, declares war on Germany. Britain is also obligated by treaty to defend Belgium. All of Britain's colonies (Australia, Canada, India, New Zealand, Union of South Africa) offer military and financial support to Britain.

August 23, 1914—Japan, which is allied with Britain, declares war on Germany.
May, 1915—Italy, which had remained neutral, joins the war and sides with the Allies.
April 6, 1917—The United States finally joins the war on the side of the Allies.

In order to better understand the conditions and limitations of World War I and to fully comprehend the role of the animals, it is important to appreciate the equipment on which the soldiers had to rely. They include communications, weapons, and warships.

COMMUNICATIONS

The two primary means of communication for ground forces during World War I were telephones and carrier pigeons, although dogs and human runners were used, too. Telephone communication was limited because physical lines had to be laid for the telephones to work. If the lines were bombed, cut, or otherwise broken, communication was lost. Each time a unit moved, new lines had to be laid. This was risky because the soldiers who had the job of laying lines were prime targets.

Airedale, trained by Major Richardson, laying phone wire. Richardson was instrumental in developing a war dog program for England and training dogs for war.

The major limitation with carrier pigeons was that they could only be trained to go to a known position, which was usually a base or headquarters. Therefore, they typically flew from the front lines to the rear and always only point to point.

Messenger dogs, however, could be trained to report back and forth from one handler to another, which allowed them to travel both ways—front to rear and rear to front. Dogs were a much more difficult target for the enemy to shoot because they could run fast and leap over craters.

Human runners were the least effective means of communication because they were slow and therefore were easy targets. However, they were the main means of communication in the trenches.

WEAPONS

The major weapons used in World War I were bolt-action rifles, machine guns that needed four to six men to work them, and field guns that were similar to cannons. The blimp or zeppelin was used to drop bombs, and tanks were introduced for the first time. Planes were also used for the first time to drop bombs and were later armed with machine guns and small cannons.

Chemical weapons in the form of gas were first used extensively in World War I. When troops were firmly dug into their trenches, attacking them was difficult using other weapons. Gas was therefore used mainly to gain control in trench warfare.

Tear gas is used today for riot control. "Tear gas" is a generic term for a group of chemicals that will temporarily disable people by causing irritation to the eyes, mouth, throat, lungs, and skin. A victim of tear gas will react within seconds of being exposed to it, but the effects are short-lived—typically less than an hour. However, prolonged exposure to tear gas, especially in an enclosed area where there is an extremely high concentration of the gas, can cause permanent damage.

Mustard gas was one of the most lethal gases used in World War I. Symptoms did not occur immediately; in most cases, it took up to twelve hours for them to develop. The gas caused a soldier's eyes to become sore, and he would start to vomit. Skin blistering led to external bleeding. The real damage, however, occurred internally. The mucous membranes in the bronchial tubes were stripped and the soldier would bleed internally. The pain was so excruciating that it was often necessary to tie the soldier to his bed. Unfortunately, it took up to five weeks for the soldier to die.

Major Richardson and two ambulance Bloodhounds.

Only small amounts of gas were required to kill soldiers, and once the gas was in the soil it could stay active for weeks. Therefore, a soldier would only have to touch the contaminated soil and suffer symptoms of exposure. This also affected the animals that came into contact with the contaminated soil.

Chlorine gas was another lethal weapon. It destroyed the respiratory organs and caused a slow death by asphyxiation.

Phosgene gas produced the same symptoms as exposure to chlorine gas—soldiers would literally choke to death. The gas damaged the skin, eyes, nose, throat, and lungs.

Although gas masks were designed for the animals that served in World War I, animals still suffered from the gases. Tear gas did not seem to bother dogs or equines as much as it did humans. The other gases, however, were a different matter. Because mustard gas remained in the soil for weeks, horses suffered lesions of the skin, especially in places where they sweated and around their hooves and where harnesses rubbed when the horses were driven through areas that had been bombed with the gas. If the animals ate food that was contaminated by mustard gas, they suffered internally. Both dogs and equines died from gas poisoning.

WARSHIPS: BATTLES AT SEA

According to Dwight Messimer, World War I historian, a major naval war took place while the soldiers fought on land.

German U-boats were considered a second front; about 200 were deployed. The British deployed a sizable fleet of submarines in the Baltic and North seas to sink the U-boats. On the home front and in the North Sea, the British deployed more than 1,000 ships to hunt for and sink U-boats.

The United States, British, French, and Japanese navies launched about 200 warships, with the United States deploying the bulk of its destroyer force in European waters.

Often overlooked, the battles at sea were a critical part of the war effort. Much of the supplies that the soldiers needed to fight and survive were shipped by sea, therefore convoys were a prime target for the German U-Boats. These supplies not only included food, arms and medical equipment, but animals as well. Many of the horses and other draft animals were shipped from the United States. All of the convoys needed naval escorts and protection making the job of the sailor a risky one.

CHAPTER 2

THE ANIMALS: A BRIEF HISTORY

Most of the animals used in World War I were dogs, mules, horses, and carrier pigeons. However, oxen, camels, elephants, cats, goats, rats, pigs, and even geese were used in war efforts or were kept as mascots.

Animals played a key role in World War I, according to Peter Shaw Baker in his book *Animal War Heroes* (1933). In 1917, on all fronts, more than one million animals were involved in World War I, and almost half of them were used in France. All types of animals also accompanied soldiers as mascots even though they were not specifically trained for military use.

Although animals have always been used in wars (records of war animals go as far back as the ancient Egyptians, Romans, and Greeks), in modern times, the Germans were training dogs as early as 1884, when they formed the first military school for training war dogs in Lechernich, near Berlin. At this school, Collies were trained to find wounded soldiers. Prior to World War I, Lieutenant Colonel Edwin Hautenville Richardson from England learned about these dogs and spent considerable time in Germany studying how the dogs were trained. It is interesting to note that, prior to World War I, the Germans preferred to use Scotch Collies for sentry and ambulance work (the Scotch Collie is today's Border Collie).

Richardson purchased a Collie named Sanita to bring back to England. Sanita was trained to lie down next to a wounded solider until help arrived, and she carried a small packet on her vest with medical supplies for the soldier to use. Shortly after bringing Sanita back to England, Richardson had a small band of Collies trained to find wounded soldiers. This was necessary because a wounded soldier would often drag himself into hiding, making him difficult for the medics to find.

The dogs had small packs on their backs that contained medical supplies, food, and brandy. After the soldier used the supplies, the dog would return to the stretcher bearers (today's medics) and lead them to the wounded man. Richardson notes that only the most intelligent dogs could perform the entire process, but all of the dogs could be taught to find the wounded soldiers.

In 1904, the Russo-Japanese War broke out, and Richardson was asked to provide two ambulance or Red Cross dogs for use in the Russian Army. These dogs were so successful that Richardson went on to train sentry dogs as well. His principal breed of choice was the Scottish Collie. Richardson's Scottish Collies were any Collie-type dog, but most were from the border regions of Scotland and Wales.

When World War I broke out, Richardson was enthusiastic about training dogs for war efforts and establishing a school in England. It is difficult to understand why, but the War Department did not embrace the use of dogs immediately, even though leaders knew that the Germans had about 30,000 dogs ready for use.

At the beginning of the war, the British army had only a handful of Airedales, which had been trained by Richardson. Because there were no official military dogs, officers from the front would contact Richardson requesting that he send them sentry and patrol dogs. At first, Richardson was able to supply dogs

The first trained ambulance Collies, trained by Richardson for the 1904–1905 Russo-Japanese War.

from his own kennels, but as the dogs succeeded in their jobs, more requests came for trained dogs. Finally the War Department endorsed the idea and a school for war dogs was established at Shoeburyness.

Many European countries were now purchasing the Collies for training, and it became difficult to find enough Collies to meet the demand. As a result, Richardson started to experiment with all breeds and finally settled on the Airedale and Bloodhound, as well as the Scottish Collie, for use as war dogs. He also used Lurchers, which were a cross between any breed (usually a Collie) and a hound, such as a Deerhound.

German soldier with dog.

Training camp for war dogs.

A sentry dog in the midst of war.

Major Richardson with one of his first Airedales

As this demand for dogs continued to increase, it became impossible to find dogs for training, and Richardson had to find other sources to supply the dogs. He recruited dogs from the Homes for Lost Dogs at Battersea, Birmingham, Liverpool, Bristol, and Manchester. These were the equivalent of today's shelters. When he ran out of dogs from these sources, the police all over England were instructed to capture all suitable stray dogs and send them to Richardson's school.

Finally these sources dried up, and the War Department appealed to the public to donate their beloved pets. Citizens overwhelming responded, and some dogs came with letters from their owners. An example of one letter stated, "I have given my husband and my sons, and now that he too is required, I give my dog" (Shaw, *Animal War Heroes*, 160).

CHAPTER 3

THE DOGS

Dogs played a vital role in World War I. They served as messenger and sentry dogs, transported carrier pigeons, carried all kinds of supplies including medical provisions that were used by wounded soldiers in the field, led the wounded to field hospitals, laid telephone wires, and served as mascots, which would be equivalent to the role of therapy dogs today.

A war dog receiving a medal for valor.

Just as in wars since World War I, the dogs endeared themselves to their human partners and have been given places of honor. Richardson's admiration for the dogs is expressed in the following:

> I felt a very personal interest in Scott—a fine Collie whose appearance was so striking that everyone was apt to "make a fuss over him;" also in Molly, the insignificant little black Lurcher who went with him, "and takes no notice of the guns or anything;" of Old Tray, and Joseph, and Swallow; of Joe and Lizzard; of Tom, who had been gassed and got a bit of shrapnel, but was all right again; of Jim, who was sent up and did a journey in seventeen minutes, which would have taken a man three-quarters of an hour. . . . There were Whitefoot, Prince, Paddy, and Mom; Blueboy, who did splendid work at Kemmel, and was finally killed in Nieppe Forest; and Creamy and Ginger, two delightfully intelligent cross-bred Lurchers . . . . I may say that Swankie's bitch Creamy helped a London regiment from being cut off on the right of Villers-Bretonneux. She and Tweed kept the battalion in touch with Brigade Headquarters. There was no way of getting a message through, only by runner or a dog, and the dog kept the way opened" (Richardson, *Fifty Years With Dogs*, 68).

Richardson goes on to describe Tweed as "a fine, large, gray, rough-coated English Sheepdog. His demeanor in war always seemed to me to be typically British, carrying, as it did, a quiet dignity; nor was there any desire to quarrel."

Just as England resisted the idea of having a school to train war dogs, so did France. Finally the French War Dog Service was established after the hostilities started. According to Ernest Harold Baynes, in his book *Animal Heroes of the Great War* (page 140), the acceptance of war dogs was due mostly to the efforts of Sergeant Paul Mégnin, who was to France what Richardson was to England.

AMBULANCE OR RED CROSS DOGS

The use of ambulance dogs was not as practical as the use of messenger dogs, only because the enemy would mistake them for messenger or ammunition dogs and shoot them on sight. Therefore, as the war progressed, more dogs were trained for other jobs. However, the ambulance dogs did save many lives. The use of ambulance dogs was not new, because prior to World War I, the Germans trained dogs to assist in finding the wounded. Some accounts of the field tests described next show how good these dogs were.

A report by Prince Adolf of Schaumburg-Lippe, who held a night trial in Bonn, Germany, to demonstrate the usefulness of the ambulance dogs, tells how his dogs found men who would have been missed by soldiers looking for them.

In another night trial held by the Army Corps at Coblentz, France (July 27, 1899), 200 soldiers were put in a large area to represent the wounded. About 500 stretcher bearers were sent out and were allowed to use torches and lanterns to find the wounded soldiers. A number of officers followed the stretcher bearers on horseback and on foot to watch the test. Once the stretcher bearers had searched the area, four dogs were brought in to do a final sweep. The dogs found eighteen men in twenty minutes who had been missed (Richardson, *War, Police and Watch Dogs*, 79–80).

By World War I, it was clear that ambulance dogs were necessary to find wounded soldiers in the field. They could quickly locate those who were still alive and identify them for the medical corpsmen. The dogs were trained to bring a small item belonging to the soldier to the medics and then lead them back to the wounded soldier if the soldier was unable to walk. If the soldier was able, he

A corps of French ambulance dogs leaving for the front.

French ambulance dog bringing back a helmet from a wounded soldier.

A French ambulance dog helping a wounded soldier.

Medal for a French war dog.

Bouvier des Flandres ambulance dog.

would follow the dog back to the field hospital. Every dog carried some medical supplies and water for the soldier.

Four dogs stand out in their notable service as ambulance dogs: Resi, Filax, Prusco, and Yew-Yew.

RESI THE COLLIE

One notable dog was Resi, a Collie bitch who earned her fame in 1899 under the command of German officer General Von Blumenthal. The account tells how Resi was sent out into a simulated battlefield after the stretcher bearers had thoroughly searched the area for missing and wounded soldiers. Three men were still missing. She was given the command "seek wounded" and took off into the large area. Within ten minutes, she had found the three soldiers missed by the stretcher bearers. Her devotion to her job was evident in the fact that she had not been distracted by the cavalry or marching men.

Resi would even guard her handler's gear while he was some distance away tending a wounded soldier.

A Scotch Collie wearing a gas mask.

FILAX THE SHEEPDOG

Filax was a sheepdog who was considered too coarse for the dog-show world, so his owner donated him to the Red Cross. Filax is credited for saving more than 100 French soldiers by traveling numerous times over "no man's land."

PRUSCO THE WOLFHOUND MIX

After a fierce battle, one French Wolfhound mix named Prusco is credited with dragging more than 100 wounded soldiers to safety. The soldiers had fallen in brush, depressions, and craters, where Prusco found them and saved them.

YEW-YEW THE MUTT

A white, shaggy dog named Yew-Yew is credited with, over a course of two years, saving hundreds of soldiers by leading field nurses to them. She lost an ear and an eye, but despite being an easy target because of her white coat, she was wounded only once.

War dog Prusco riding a motorcycle.

French ambulance dogs.

Ambulance dog retrieving a helmet.

French ambulance dogs leaving Paris.

Ambulance dog leads medic to an unconscious man.

SENTRY DOGS

Different levels of sentry dogs were used during the war. Some were referred to as "enclosure dogs," whose duty was to guard areas such as warehouses. These dogs were turned loose when necessary to protect an enclosed area. The "rounds" dog comprised the next level. These dogs patrolled with a handler and were used to find people who might be hiding in an area. They defended the handler and also caught fleeing intruders.

The highest level of sentry dog was the "detective dog," who worked with a handler in a harness. This dog did all of the above duties as well as follow a trail, search areas for hidden people, and identify the person whose trail he had followed. These dogs were used in a harness so that they could pull as hard as they wanted in pursuit of their quarry.

Some outstanding sentry dogs were Helda, Za, Faro, Max, Polo, Cabot, Lutz, and Pyrame. Their stories come next.

HELDA AND ZA, THE GERMAN SHEPHERD DOGS

Sergeant Mégnin and an assistant brought two Alsatian Sheepdogs, Helda and Za, to the front lines to assist. (Alsatian Sheepdogs are German Shepherds. It is believed that the name was changed for psychological reasons because the Germans were the enemies at the time.) The captain in charge was doubtful about how useful they could be. However, he explained a problem that they were having locating a Boche (German) outpost at night. Sergeant Mégnin took Helda, and his assistant took Za, 150 meters down the trench line. Within ten minutes, both dogs had indicated the location of the outpost.

Troops with mascot on the way to the front.

Helda reportedly became one of the most famous sentry dogs in the French army when she was able to track down and identify a French soldier who had turned traitor. The man, Private Vachet, was a kennel assistant at the Vosges and Alsace war dog kennel and would sneak out at night to give information to the German army. Helda, who slept next to kennel man Private Herbelin, started to growl one night when Helda heard Vachet try to quiet the dogs (other dogs were growling as well). Herbelin reported this to his commanding officer, and, after a few nights of watching, they tried to follow Vachet when he slipped out of the camp. Unfortunately, they could not follow him in the dark.

The next time Vachet left the camp, Helda and another dog, El Tango, were used to follow him in order to verify his treasonous behavior. When Vachet was confronted, he denied his activities. Helda was turned loose and she attacked Vachet, who then quickly confessed to what he had been doing. What is remarkable is that all of the dogs knew and trusted Vachet, so we can only wonder how they knew he was a traitor (Baynes, *Animal Heroes of the Great War*, 143- 144).

FARO THE BEAUCERON AND MAX THE DOBERMAN—DETECTIVE DOGS

In 1916 a gang of deserters terrorized the area comprising the Department of the Saône and became involved in smuggling, stealing, and murdering. The severity of this group is illustrated by the size of the force of men assembled by the French Seventh Army to capture the outlaws. This force consisted of an infantry company of soldiers, engineers with explosives and poisonous gas, twenty-five MPs, police commissaries, secret service personnel, and the head of the Intelligence Service. Most important of all, the force included a Beauceron named Faro and a Doberman named Max. Both dogs were experienced in sentry work and were trusted by their handlers. Faro had won many police-dog trials and Max had captured poachers.

The military and police forces had a good idea that the gang was hiding in abandoned buildings located deep in the woods. They quietly surrounded the site.

Faro was sent in to search the buildings and, after exploring every inch, proved that the bandits were not there. In the meantime, Max had found a trail in the woods outside the deserted buildings and led the men to what appeared to be a deserted farmhouse. However, a man and woman were living in the house, and the

French sentry man with a sentry dog.

21

woman insisted that only her husband was there, sick in bed. Max maintained that this was one of the gang members whom he had been tracking, and after the man was interrogated, he confessed. The gang was finally caught.

POLO THE SENTRY DOG

It was common practice for the Germans to try to capture soldiers who were on sentry duty in order to coerce important information from them. However, the sentry dogs made this practice very difficult, if not impossible. An example is a dog named Polo, who warned his handler about a German patrol that was cutting the barbed-wire barrier protecting a blockhouse. The dog warned his handler by first pointing in the direction with his head and then growling.

A corps of sentry dogs.

CABOT THE BULLDOG MIX

Another famous sentry dog, named Cabot, was reported to be part Bulldog. Most sentry dogs would not leave their post/handlers, but on one occasion Cabot took off across "no-man's land" followed by his handler. Cabot found and attacked a German messenger dog, and Cabot's handler was able to retrieve a metal tube containing German dispatches.

LUTZ

Lutz, a famous dog at Verdun, was awarded the war cross star for working in advance of the troops, alerting them to the presence of the enemy.

PYRAME

A short account of a dog named Pyrame tells how he saved an entire battalion of soldiers by barking to signal the presence of a large army of Germans.

MESSENGER DOGS

The use of messenger dogs in war is not a new concept and has been mentioned in early war accounts as far back as 4000 B.C. However, at the beginning of World War I, the British military was not convinced that the dogs would be of use. They changed their mind after the War Department received the following communication from Colonel Winter, R.A.:

From O.C. 56th Brigade, Royal Field Artillery.
To R.A. Headquarters, 11th Division.
    In continuation of my letter No. 549 dated on the 7th inst., during the operations against Wytschaete Ridge, two messenger dogs attached to this Brigade were sent forward at 1 A.M. One was attached to the forward liaison officer, and one with the group forward observation officer.
    After being led up through communication trenches during darkness, they went forward as soon as the attack was launched, passing through the smoke barrage.... One was dispatched at 10:45 A.M. and the other at 12:45 P.M.
    Both dogs reached brigade headquarters, traveling a distance as the crow flies of 4,000 yards, over ground they had never seen before, and over an exceptionally difficult terrain. The dog dispatched at 12:45 P.M. reached his destination under the hour, bringing an important message, and this was the first message which was received, all visual communication having failed.
    Signed O.C. 56th Brigade, R.F.A.

A Beauceron messenger dog leaps over the trench.

The War Department received two more reports about the two messenger dogs from Colonel Winter as follows:

> When the Germans withdrew their line in the spring of 1917, the dogs were taken up the night before to a wood east of Bucquoy. They were then sent up to a forward observation post, 4,000 yards to the east of the wood, and were released with important messages. They found their way back, through masses of troops on the march, to the wood, although they had only arrived there the night previously, and the ground was quite unknown to them.
>
> On the attack on the Vimy Ridge the dogs were employed with an artillery observation post. All the telephones were broken, and visual signaling was impossible. The dogs were the first to bring through news (Richardson, *Watch Dogs: Their Training and Management*, 185).

It was mainly due to the reports of success from Colonel Winter that the British army was persuaded to establish a messenger-dog program.

In his book *Watch Dogs: Their Training and Management*, Richardson explained that the training of the messenger dog was different than any other type of training. The messenger dog had to work in a similar manner as the sheepdog, traveling great distances from the handler to do his job.

The messenger dog needed to know what he had to do, and sometimes he had to solve the problem of *how* to do it on his own. The messenger dog also needed to love what he was doing. Richardson clearly stated that training methods using coercion would not work and should not be used, which is interesting and important to today's trainers as well. The dogs were taught with what we know today as positive training methods. Richardson also made it clear that, if the dog made a mistake, he should never be chastised but should only be shown again what to do. This is the same philosophy that most search-and-rescue dog handlers use today. What Richardson explained is similar to the job of today's search-and-rescue dogs and the current training methods. Richardson illustrated that the positive training methods of today are not new. It is interesting that, by World War II, the training methods had become very harsh and harmful despite the success of the positive methods used in World War I.

Two kinds of messenger dogs were used in the war, the dog that ran back to the handler, who was stationed at a rear base, and the "liaison" dog. In the first scenario, a handler (or "keeper," as they were sometimes called) would take three

Messenger dogs in training.

dogs to battalion headquarters. A soldier would take one dog with him to the front lines. When they needed to send a message back to headquarters, a message was put in a tin cylinder attached to the dog's collar, and the dog was sent back to his handler. The liaison dog, on the other hand, would report back and forth between handlers, sometimes bringing an answer back to the soldier on the front. The British typically did not use liaison dogs.

The most important quality needed by messenger dogs was to be able to ignore the bombing and shooting. They had to be resourceful enough to overcome whatever obstacles they encountered, such as swimming through bodies of water, including shell holes filled with water; worming their way through barbed wire; and leaping over trenches and craters. They also had to stick to their mission. They could not be distracted when traveling through towns or areas where a lot of non-battle human activity was occurring, other animals were present, and food was available to eat.

According to Richardson, Collies were the best messenger dogs. He found that Greyhounds did not make good messenger dogs for long distances but noted that, when they were crossed with another breed, they were excellent. These crosses, as noted earlier, were called Lurchers. Richardson also had many good things to say about Airedales, and because of their availability, these dogs were one of the most common breeds used by the British. It is interesting to note that Richardson says, "There were a good many sheepdogs, retrievers, Irish Terriers, and spaniels; a few Deerhounds, setters, Welsh Terriers, and Bull Terriers; and a very few Greyhounds, Eskimos, Dalmatians, Bedlingtons, Pointers, Bulldogs, and Whippets. As might be guessed, the great majority of war dogs were not pure-bred. (Baynes, *Animal Heroes of the Great War*, 163).

Messenger dogs both transported information quickly, especially at night, and saved the lives of many soldiers. Pigeons could not be used at night, and thus the job went to the dogs.

According to Baynes, the casualties for messenger dogs were very low considering the dangers of the job. The British discovered that the messenger dogs could travel three or four miles between handlers and were successful at intervals of up to twelve hours. If the dog was sent for longer than twelve hours, the success rate diminished.

Contrary to what people might think, Richardson felt that hounds were useless as messenger dogs because they were untrainable. Richardson claimed that a hound would lose interest in the job after a mile in distance. Richardson also believed that dogs that carried their tails over their back or to the side were

A British messenger Border Collie with the tube around his neck.

26

useless as well. He felt that they were not serious working dogs (Baker, *Animal War Heroes*, 40–41; Baynes, *Animal Heroes of the Great War*, 163).

Messenger dogs faced some daunting situations in their work. According to the official report on the work of the dogs at Kemmel (Belgium):

> It is of interest to note that these dogs did sterling work between Kemmel and Scherpenberg [Belgium], during the whole of the German attack on Kemmel Hill. . . . Two out of the twelve dogs were badly wounded, and all the dogs suffered from the gas, although they ultimately recovered.
>
> Exceptionally good work was done by these dogs through the forest of Nieppe, and interest in the messenger dogs, as a means of communication in heavily shelled areas, was aroused.
>
> After the Armistice, I again made an entire and close inspection of the entire battlefield, with the object of studying the various sorts of surfaces the messenger dogs had to traverse. The Ypres sector is, of course, one of the worst, and in its shell-torn ground the dogs must have had all their energies called out. In wet weather, when every step brought a risk of drowning in the terrific shell holes to the human runner—and this apart from the ceaseless firing—a message would

A Border Collie messenger dog leaping over shell holes.

27

A French messenger dog leaping over the trenches.

have a far greater chance of being brought through safely by a dog. If the dog fell into a hole, it could easily swim and scramble out, and it would certainly be able to negotiate these obstacles much more quickly, creeping lightly along the lip of the craters.

At Passchendaele [Belgium] also, the terrible slope presented unending dangers to anyone forced to move rapidly, and here, too, excellent work was done by the dogs, which would have been appallingly difficult, if not impossible to runners. Other parts of the line presented different features, but in every sector, I came to the conclusion that message carrying could be carried out with far greater dispatch and certainty (Richardson, *Watch Dogs: Their Training and Management*, 211–213).

Next are some stories of extraordinary messenger dogs.

MICHAEL (MIKE) THE AIREDALE

Mike, trained by Colonel Richardson, was the first dog to serve as an English messenger dog in World War I. Mike was assigned to the advancing

28

forces in France, and his job was to bring messages from the advancing forces back to headquarters. Once he reached headquarters, he was sent back to the advancing forces. Mike was constantly under fire as he ran from one location to the other. Mike was fortunate that he was never wounded, although he was gassed, which left him nervous and with his vision slightly impaired.

When the forces were demobilized, Captain R.R. Slater brought Mike (by airplane) back to England, where he lived the rest of his life—to a ripe old age of sixteen. Mike never forgot what it was like being in war and for the rest of his life would crouch or hide whenever he heard a loud bang; otherwise he was a happy dog.

A messenger Airedale being sent with a communiqué.

DICK THE RETRIEVER MIX

The devotion of the messenger dogs is illustrated in the account of a black retriever cross named Dick. While he was transporting a message, he was badly wounded in the back and shoulder, yet, despite his wounds, he delivered his message. He was sent to the veterinarian for care, healed nicely, and returned to duty. A few days after he went back to the front, he became lame. It was finally determined that he had a bullet lodged between his shoulder and the wall of his chest. He also had a shell splinter in the small of his back, which was very close to his spine.

TWEED THE BOBTAILED SHEEPDOG

Tweed, a bobtailed sheepdog, earned fame for his work in France. Reports show that Tweed was at first considered a "dunce" at the war-dog school. Major Richardson's wife took an interest in the dog and discovered that his problem was shyness. She worked with him, and he went on to become one of the most reliable messenger dogs in the British army.

According to the account of his heroism:

> Tweed went on duty with a Scottish Canadian regiment at Amiens in 1918. The Germans broke through and cut off the British front line, and had they gone but a little further would probably have captured the town. Three dogs were sent to the headquarters of the French Colonial, 3 kilometers back, with the message: "Send up reinforcement and small round ammunition." Tweed ran through the German barrage and arrived in ten minutes, and the French were sent up. They straightened out the lines and saved Amiens from the Germans. Tweed became so well known that units would request him, and he never faltered in his service (author archives).

LITTLE JIM THE MIXED BREED

Another famous British messenger dog was a highly unusual mix named Little Jim. He was a cross between a retriever and a Pomeranian! The soldiers who saw him run his messages were amazed at how fast he was for a little dog. One soldier, when asked to describe Little Jim, said, "I didn't really see a dog at all. I just saw a black streak across the shell-torn ground, and the men shouted, 'There goes Little Jim!'" Little Jim was never gassed or shot in his career and remained a popular messenger dog.

PADDY

A remarkable account involves a dog named Paddy. On his first mission, he was gassed so badly that he had to spend three weeks in the hospital. On his next and second mission, after being released from the hospital, he was gassed again. No one knows how he made it back to headquarters, but he was found lying in his kennel completely blind. He was sent back to the hospital, where he fully recovered. On another mission, he was shot by a German and was left for dead. Again, he somehow crawled back to headquarters and "reported." The records do not show his final fate.

SATAN THE LURCHER

The French used both types of messenger dogs, called "estafettes" and "liaison" dogs. In one of the fiercest battles at Verdun, seventeen human runners were killed when their unit was cut off. They had only one liaison dog, Satan, who was their final hope because the last homing pigeon had been killed and no man could get through the German barrage.

Satan was a Lurcher—a Greyhound and a herding champion Collie mix. Not only did Satan make it to the unit that was cut off with an important message of hope, but he returned with two homing pigeons in cages on his back. Badly wounded, he managed to drag himself into the arms of his waiting handler. The pigeons were released with information about where the German battery was located. One pigeon was shot immediately, but shortly after, the French artillery started to shell the German battery. The other pigeon had made it with the message, giving the artillery unit the location of the battery.

Wounded comrades of war.

VON KLUCK

Sometimes the enemy's dogs were captured and retrained. One such dog was named Von Kluck by the French. He was a great messenger dog and on one mission was bombed and thrown several feet into the air. He lay there for about ten seconds while the soldiers watched him, thinking he was dead or wounded. They were surprised and happy when he got up, shook himself, and finished his mission.

BOUÉE

Bouée was a small, fuzzy, dirty, yellow-and-black dog without a tail. He was cited on three different occasions à l'ordre de l'armèe for his services. His last citation was a result of his work as a messenger dog under extremely heavy fire when all telephone connections had been destroyed. The citation read: "Bouée No Mle 1375A – Chine de liaison of the first order; fulfilling his duties in a perfect manner of the Xme Régt. D'Infanterie. During a very violent bombardment at each shell explosion the animal crouched to the ground and then immediately afterward continued his way to his destination. Absolutely remarkable for his regularity and his quickness; nor does he allow anything to distract him when he is given a duty" (author archives).

LITTLE JIM THE RETRIEVER/SPANIEL MIX

Many dogs had the same name during World War I, and so it can be confusing to determine which story goes with a particular dog. This Little Jim was a black cross between a retriever and a spaniel. His official number was "Dog 36."

According to his handler's report, Jim earned the commanding officer's commendation; the commanding officer also felt that Jim was by far the finest dog in France. Jim's handler, Private Osbourne, reported that when Jim was on an offensive in Belgium, he carried messages under heavy shell fire in record time. Another time when Jim was in the trenches, he gave the soldiers warnings of gas attacks. Osbourne noted that Jim was sent to warn headquarters about the gas attack and reached headquarters a full fifteen minutes before the wire message arrived. When a gas attack occurred, the soldiers would put Jim's head in a soldier's smoke helmet or mask (Richardson, *Watch Dogs: Their Training and Management*, 201).

NELL THE COLLIE

Another account describes a show Collie named Nell that was sable and white, sensitive, and highly strung. As Richardson states in *Watch Dogs: Their Training and Management* (page 205), "...to look at her one would have thought there was no room in her narrow skull for brains." She turned out to be a wonderful messenger dog and saved hundreds of lives. She was a reliable, steady dog until the end of the war. She survived and enjoyed retirement with her handler.

Nell, a famous British messenger Collie.

GINGER

The dogs, like the soldiers, sometimes suffered from shell shock. One account of a dog named Ginger, who was a good messenger dog, tells how she became shell-shocked for a while but went on to recover. She continued her service without a problem.

CREAMY

Reports like the following one are common regarding the accomplishments of messenger dogs during World War I:

> The last time this Division (18th) was in action, I was sent to Brigade Headquarters. After being there for one night, my dog "Creamy" was taken out during an attack and carried a map of ---- also a message from the front-line trenches back to Brigade Headquarters. Time taken was 25 minutes, whereas a man took from two and a half to three hours. Under the conditions and heavy shell fire, it was very good, and my officers were highly pleased with it, for the map and message were very important and all other means of communication at the time failed (Richardson, *Watch Dogs: Their Training and Management*, 207).

A Bully mascot.

It is obvious that the messenger dogs faced many distractions and obstacles in their runs, yet their devotion to their jobs and their sense of duty never cease to amaze.

BOXER THE AIREDALE AND FLASH THE LURCHER

Boxer, an Airedale, and Flash, a Lurcher, were assigned to the 34th Division and carried messages through mud that came up to their bellies. Boxer was especially fast; he could deliver a message in the belly-deep mud over a distance of four miles in twenty-five minutes. A man would have taken two hours.

Dixon, Boxer's and Flash's handler, further reported that his two dogs were doing very well in the field. He described Boxer as running like an engine and that Flash was even faster by twenty minutes.

However, even the best dog can be tempted. One day Boxer took longer than usual to make his run because he stopped to eat a carcass. Dixon related that, when Boxer returned from his run, he tried to sneak back into his bed. Dixon believed that Boxer did this because he knew he had been wrong. It was not unusual for a field to have rubbish, carcasses, abandoned cookhouses, and miscellaneous debris in them.

JACK THE AIREDALE; WHITEFOOT AND LLOYD, WELSH TERRIERS

Another report by a handler named Errington explains how his three dogs, Jack (an Airedale), and Whitefoot and Lloyd (two large Welsh Terriers), had to work through a place called Strazeele (in northern France) with roads that had a lot of human traffic, stray dogs, dead cattle, sheep, and poultry (killed by the shelling). The dogs ran five kilos in about forty-five minutes.

PADDY THE IRISH TERRIER AND ROMAN THE COLLIE

A handler called MacLeod tells of Irish Terrier "Paddy" who was gassed, wounded, and left for dead, yet showed up at headquarters with his message. This same handler tells about a purebred, tri-colored Collie named Roman who was a show-quality dog with a beautiful flowing coat and narrow head (the Lassie-type Collie). During training, Roman appeared very self-centered and took his time to cover the distance he had to travel, but he showed a remarkable ability to analyze the situation and work it to the best advantage. Roman proved to be very devoted to his job and had a keen sense of right and wrong.

BLUE BOY THE BEDLINGTON TERRIER

A report by a handler named Matheson describes Blue Boy, a Bedlington Terrier who did an outstanding job at Mount Kemmel. He delivered his message under intense machine-gun fire.

BOBBY THE SHEEPDOG MIX

It was not uncommon for the armies of both sides of the war to capture animals with prisoners. Often the armies would adopt the animal and put it to use. Such was the case with Bobby and Max. It is interesting to note that almost every account of a captured dog by the Allies mentions the high intelligence of the dogs captured from the Germans. It is often mentioned how quickly the dogs adapted to their new master and the speed with which they responded to commands.

Bobby was captured with German prisoners in 1915 and was adopted by the Royal Sussex Regiment. He is described as being large and strong, having a shaggy coat, and being very clever.

Bobby served as a messenger dog for a number of months in the trenches with the regiment. However, during a very heavy battle, he disappeared. The soldiers had become very fond of him and mourned his loss. None of the soldiers knew exactly what happened to Bobby.

In October 1916, a chateau near Etaples in northern France was converted into a field hospital. Hundreds of men came through on a regular basis. One group of wounded men happened to be from the Royal Sussex, and they were placed in a ward with other wounded soldiers.

One of the men saw a large, shaggy dog walking through the ward, stopping at each bed to greet the soldiers with a friendly wag. The man recognized the dog as Bobby and called to him. Bobby instantly stopped and then ran to the soldier, barking with joy.

After that, Bobby inspected every group of wounded soldiers and found some of his other comrades. However, Bobby's job was not finished. In April 1917, the hospital was bombed by airplanes, and all of the wounded were rushed to the cellars of the chateau, which had not been used for years. Like most buildings of that time, the cellars were infested with rats. These rats were not afraid of humans and would bite the wounded men, especially those who could not defend themselves. Almost immediately, Bobby caught and killed all of the rats and kept the cellars rat free for the rest of the time the soldiers were kept in the cellars.

The mystery of how Bobby wound up at the field hospital was solved when a nurse explained that she originally had seen Bobby wandering around as if lost and brought him to the hospital. After awhile, Bobby was returned to his regiment, where he resumed his work as a messenger dog.

When the war ended, he was sent to England, where he was adopted and had a peaceful, happy life.

MAX THE SMOOTH COLLIE MIX

Max served with three armies. He started as a Russian messenger/sentry dog but was captured by the Germans and then by the British. He understood commands in all three languages. He also had special training so that he could grab an intruder either on the arm or leg but not bite hard enough to puncture the skin unless commanded to do so.

After the war, Max was taken to London, where he was adopted by an ex-officer.

The messenger dog and message tube.

NAMES AND BREEDS OF SOME OF THE FIRST MESSENGER DOGS

In his book *Watch Dogs: Their Training and Management*, Richardson listed some of the first messenger dogs. It is interesting to note that all but four were males and that many different breeds were successfully trained to be messenger dogs.

Breed	Name
Airedale	Buller
Collie	Trick
Setter	Nell
Collie Lurcher	Yellow
Airedale	Rocket
Airedale	Jame
Airedale	Tags
Old English Sheepdog	Tweed
Retriever	Lill
Irish Terrier	Paddy
Irish Terrier	Mick
Irish (missing)	Cocoa
Airedale	Dale
Airedale Lurcher	Badger
Bloodhound (missing)	Duke
Retriever sheepdog	Curly
Airedale Irish	Gyp
Irish (missing)	Dick
Lurcher	Sharp
Irish Water Spaniel	Coffee
Yellow Lurcher	Vulcan
Lurcher	Dan
Retriever	Black Petal
Collie	Flight
Terrier	Georgie
Spaniel	Spotty
Retriever	Hanky
Brown Setter	Ginger
Collie	Ben
Airedale	Moses
Lurcher	Frolic

Collie	Willard
Spaniel	Drummer
Collie	Jim
Old Sheepdog	Jock
Bedlington	Dick
Irish Bedlington	Paddy
Brown Lurcher	Lady
Lurcher	Roger
Small Retriever	Darkie
Retriever Spaniel	Prince
Collie	Flier
Whippet	Skim
Irish	Links
Whippet	Forest
Lurcher	Slick
Collie Lurcher	Rapid
Lurcher	Sailor

Richardson also listed the number of dogs trained successfully in one month's time:

Collies	74
Lurchers	70
Airedales	66
Sheepdogs	36
Retrievers	33
Irish Terriers	18
Spaniels	11
Deerhounds	6
Setters	4
Welsh Terriers	5
Bull Terriers	5
Greyhounds	2
Eskimos	2
Dalmatians	2
Bedlingtons	2
Pointers	2
Bulldogs	1
Whippets	1

Richardson noted that some of the breeds worked very well but did not have a large representation because they were not readily available for use by the military. He especially liked the Welsh Terriers, but few were available for training (*Watch Dogs: Their Training and Management*, 195, 196).

TRANSPORT OR PACK DOGS

In a number of European countries, such as Belgium, Holland, Switzerland, and northern France, dogs had been used as carting dogs long before World War I. A modern example of these dogs is the Greater Swiss Mountain Dog and the Bernese Mountain Dog, which were bred primarily as carting dogs.

In the countries where the carting dogs were popular, laws were established about the type of cart and harness that could be used. The proper equipment allowed the dog to pull about 500 pounds, and a brace could pull up to half a ton. They could pull that much weight because the weight of the material rested on the well-balanced cart wheels instead of on the dog's shoulders.

The same types of carts and harnesses were used in battle situations. In battle, an officer would pick a position for a machine gun, then another soldier would advance to that position with the dog cart. The soldiers would off-load the gun, tripod and all, and set it into firing position while the dogs were led to a rear, sheltered position.

The Belgian army used about 500 dogs divided into twelve companies. Because the dogs were right on the front lines, many were killed or wounded. However, in the rear of the front lines, veterinary hospitals cared for sick or wounded dogs. The carting dogs were taught to lie down on command, to go, to stop, and to get up.

Transport dogs bring ammunition to the front.

A mascot accompanies the troops on a march behind the lines.

On a lighter note, some of the carting dogs were used to sell war bonds. One such group was headed by Lieutenant Joseph Scheppers of the 7th Regiment, Belgian army. It consisted of ten dogs with their carts, guns, and water carts. This group attended many parades, and the dogs were fussed over. On one occasion, a dog named Bamboula barked at a lady who tried to pet him. When she asked Lieutenant Scheppers why Bamboula did that, he smiled and told her that the dog wanted her to buy a bond, which, in the sport of the event, she did.

The Italian army employed about 3,500 transport/carting/pack dogs in the Alps to move material and ammunition. These dogs were larger Saint Bernard–type dogs that typically weighed 125 to 150 pounds. They were red and white and had very heavy coats so that they could withstand the cold—very similar to today's Saint Bernard.

In areas that were too steep for any other animal to travel, the dogs would carry the supplies in packs on their backs. The canine transport groups were usually comprised of thirty to thirty-five dogs with one handler. The dogs were trained much the same as mules; they were taught on command to go right or left at a fork in the trail. "Gee" meant to go right, and "haw" meant to go left. Sled dogs were also taught to go right or left on command using those same commands. Each dog's load of supplies weighed about sixty pounds.

The pack dogs were responsible for bringing soldiers supplies that other animals could not deliver. An example of how important these dogs were is explained by Lieutenant Hautecloque: "The average load consisted of fifteen grenades, or fifteen machine-gun belts per dog. Each dog made six trips a day, which means on certain days the supply of over 400 loads of ammunition by dogs." (Each squad consisted of five men and twenty-four dogs.)

Of course, the dogs that carried warm soup and food to the men in the trenches were often the most welcomed!

The transport/pack/carting dogs also helped civilians escape from the war zone by transporting their household goods, food, and sometimes the young and elderly. Although this was not a "war" job, and these were privately owned dogs and not dogs of war, their jobs were equally important.

French transport dog bringing food to the troops.

Transport dog pulls a funeral cart.

PRISON DOGS

The use of guard dogs at POW camps was not favorably looked upon by the Allies. This was because the French had officially protested the use of prison dogs by the Germans, who freely used them to guard prisoners of war. However, a few dogs were unofficially used at the prison in Dijon prior to 1918. It did not take long for the French to change their mind about the use of guard dogs, and they started to employ them.

CAPORAL

Caporal, a guard dog, was mentioned by Baynes in *Animal Heroes of the Great War* (1925). A prisoner tried to escape by pretending to pick wildflowers during an exercise period. Caporal went after the man without being commanded by his handler, bit the man in the thigh, and drove him back to the column. Another time, four prisoners escaped. The guards caught three of them and, after being scented on the fourth prisoner's trail, Caporal tracked and caught the last man (Baynes, 197).

TSEKOFF

On his first night of duty, Tsekoff discovered two spies hiding in a flour wagon. He attacked them and did quite a bit of damage (Baynes, 197).

SLED DOGS

Sled dogs also aided soldiers in the Great War, because soldiers were stationed in the Alps and fought the same kinds of battles as other troops in the rest of Europe.

The dogs were used to haul sleds in the winter with up to 250 pounds of food and supplies. The sleds were similar to the freight sleds used in Alaska. They had a step in the back where the driver could ride and handles so that the driver could help the dogs by pushing the sled. Most people think of drivers as riding on the sled most of the time, but in reality, drivers ran alongside the sled or helped to push it.

During World War I, a team of soldiers on skis dressed in white led the way and the driver followed behind.

Supplies were critical to alpine soldiers, even more so because of the bitter cold in winter. The only means of getting critical supplies to the soldiers was by sled.

Sled dogs of war.

One account tells how, after a very heavy snowfall, a kennel of 150 dogs moved more than fifty tons of food and ammunition in four days. In the Vosges Mountains, more than a thousand Alaskan sled dogs helped keep the Germans at bay by supplying the troops (author's personal archives).

Another example tells of an American woman (unnamed) who brought a Croix de Guerre back to America that had been awarded by the French to her teams of Malamutes for a brave rescue they did in the French Alps. (Many dogs were imported from Alaska to Europe to be used as sled dogs.)

Huskies in the snow of Vosges.

Dead ambulance dog.

Apparently the Germans were closing in on an outpost of French soldiers. The French sent human messengers to call for help but received no response. The soldiers were trapped and overwhelmed by a howling blizzard. Lieutenant Fene Haas hitched twenty-eight of his sled dogs to a light sled and headed for headquarters to get help. They had to go down the mountain and through a dangerous pass to reach the main army post.

Shortly after they arrived, his dogs were broken down into smaller teams and hitched to fourteen light sleds (two dogs per sled). They returned through the raging blizzard, as well as through gun and artillery fire from the enemy. After five days they reached the French troops and saved the day (author's personal archives).

OTHER DOGS

Some accounts of dogs do not classify the job the dog was trained for or if it was a mascot. In some cases, after a battle, a pet dog left behind would "adopt" a particular soldier or regiment and stay with them. No one knows for sure what happened to the dog's owners. This section will tell the accounts of notable dogs.

MICHAEL

When his master was left for dead in "no man's land," Michael, on his own, dragged his owner, who was alive but unconscious, back to the trenches and saved his life.

NELLIE THE FOX TERRIER

A Fox Terrier named Nellie followed her owner through a hail of bullets and bombs at the first battle of Ypres. She was later adopted by a Belgian regiment and wounded twice by shrapnel but never refused to "go over the hill." Nellie lived out her days in America after being brought over by a Belgian missionary.

DOGS THAT LED THE BLIND

Although some dogs were trained to lead soldiers who had lost their sight in the war, this was not favorably looked upon. People at that time felt that a blind man who was led by a dog would be viewed as someone who needed charity.

The dogs that were trained to lead the blind were taught with similar techniques that are used today. It took about two months to train the average dog, and for those who were very smart, training took only six weeks.

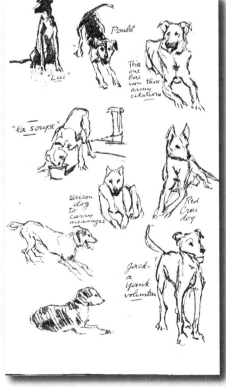

Sketches by C. LeRoy Baldridge of war dogs.

Sultane

E. The pouch with messages

Caprice

a sentinel dog

Filon

"Le Soupe"

Saïd

Capitaine

The accounts of the war dogs is a testimony to their loyalty, devotion and ability to perform whatever task was asked of them. It is amazing to think of how these courageous animals did not waver from their jobs despite being injured, hungry and sometimes separated from their handlers. Today we have a better understanding of how intelligent dogs are. We know that they are able to make decisions based on past and present experiences and plan for the future, but people during World War I did not have the scientific proof that we have today. However, in their hearts they knew, and believed in their canine comrades.

46

CHAPTER 4

THE PIGEONS

THE MANY VALIANT FEATS OF WARTIME BIRDS

During the Franco–Prussian war (1870–1871), which only lasted for four months, pigeons carried 150,000 official dispatches and 1,000,000 private messages. Although this was not the first time that pigeons were used to send messages, it was during this war that they earned their status as a successful means of communication and paved the way for the pigeon service in World War I.

The pigeons were so good at their job of delivering messages that in World War I they were recognized as a weapon of war. As soon as the Germans occupied Belgium or any other area, they ordered the execution of all pigeons. Anyone caught with one was punished for possessing war contraband.

The pigeons used as messenger birds were not the typical wild pigeons found in most city parks. They were specially bred in Belgium, chiefly in the cities of Liège, Verviers, Brussels, and Antwerp.

This type of pigeon was bred to travel long distances and, according to Baynes (*Animal Heroes of the Great War*, 1925), was not a carrier pigeon, which was developed in Baghdad and used for short flights of up to 100 miles. The pigeons used in World War I were homing pigeons and became known as racing pigeons that could fly for fifteen hours at a time. In good weather, with the proper handling and care (in peacetime), the birds were known to fly 500 miles—some up to 800 and a few up to 1,000 miles.

The pigeons in World War I often traveled at sixty miles per hour. In one case, going with the wind, a pigeon was clocked going thirty-eight miles in twenty minutes, which is equal to 114 miles per hour.

However, war conditions were far from ideal because the birds had to brave all weather conditions as well as poisonous gases and enemy fire.

Just as Colonel Richardson and M. Mégnin were the champions of war dogs, Lieutenant-Colonel A.H. Osman, OBE, was the director of the British Pigeon Service (Baynes, *Animal Heroes of the Great War*, 207).

Osman established a volunteer unit to use pigeons as a means of communication for ships that did not have wireless capabilities. The birds were also released from aircraft. This may seem impossible to us in modern times, but it is understandable when we realize that the aircraft of the day could not travel fast. Depending upon the type of aircraft, the speed ranged from 75 to about 120 miles per hour.

The birds were especially useful on seaplanes, because if a seaplane landed on the water it lost its wireless capabilities. Training a bird to go home from the sea was complicated, but eventually the success rate improved and only about 3 percent of the birds got lost. Another problem with using birds on seaplanes was

Releasing a pigeon from an airplane.

that the cockpit on the plane was small and there was no room for pigeon cages. Eventually the birds were housed in a container on the float of the plane.

In war situations dogs and pigeons were the primary means of communication. Pigeons had advantages over dogs in that they could fly high above gunfire, they were not hindered by the mud and other obstacles on the ground, they were fast, they could fly much farther than a dog could run (the typical dog was good for up to four miles), and they were much smaller targets for gunfire. However, they did suffer from mustard gas and shrapnel from bombs. Keep in mind, though, how small a pigeon is and how fast it could fly. Hitting one with a rifle was very difficult and mostly a result of plain luck. Even though pigeons had some edge over dogs, together they made a good team. Messenger dogs were sometimes used to transport pigeons to the front lines.

Baynes comments that, in the Battle of the Somme, more than 5,000 pigeons were used by the French army and only 2 percent failed to return to their lofts (*Animal Heroes of the Great War*, 213).

Richardson with an Airedale trained to carry pigeons.

British receiving pigeons on the back of a dog.

Pigeons carried their messages in a variety of ways. The most common and well known were light aluminum cylinders that were attached to the pigeon's leg. The message was put into the smaller cylinder that was then fit into a larger one and secured to the pigeon's leg with a band. Sometimes messages were put into small, soft leather pouches that were buttoned around the bird's leg. Other messages were put in a sort of a knapsack that fit on the bird's breast and were held on with rubber bands. The knapsack was used for longer messages such as maps, sketches, and up to fifteen feet of film. In a pinch, messages would be placed directly on the bird's leg and attached with a rubber band.

The pigeons were trained to return to a specific place, usually at the rear of the fighting zone. However, these sites had to relocate as the front lines moved. It would take the pigeons a few days to learn the locale of their new temporary home. When they were once again reliable, they could return to their message-delivery tasks.

The military had mobile pigeon lofts that were built on the back of a truck. The mobile lofts made it easier to transport and teach a large number of pigeons

Mobile pigeon loft.

at the same time. The fact that the pigeons only took a couple of days to acclimate themselves to a new location demonstrates their intelligence as well as their ability to remember their surroundings. There is no record of a pigeon going to a former location by mistake.

Unfortunately it was not uncommon for pigeons to be wounded during their flight. Typically they would lose a leg or an eye. According to Baynes, if a pigeon's wings were not damaged, the bird would still deliver the message and return home even though it was wounded (*Animal Heroes of the Great War*, 216). The story of Cher Ami, later in this chapter, is a striking example of this kind of courage.

By the end of the Great War the American Pigeon Service had nine officers, 324 soldiers, 6,000 pigeons, and fifty mobile pigeon lofts.

Baynes says that the air force did not use pigeons as often as did the troops on the ground, mostly because they had wireless capabilities and pilots were not able to fly the airplanes and write messages to attach to the pigeons at the same time. The airplanes of World War I did not have autopilot, and, because they were small, they had to be driven as diligently as an automobile. However, pilots did experiment with the birds and found that they could release a bird as high as 6,000 feet and still have the bird return home (*Animal Heroes of the Great War*, 223).

Sometimes a pigeon would be released from an airplane and later the plane would be shot down or captured. The pigeon often gave the ground troops the last observation of the lost plane.

Pigeons were especially useful if a seaplane had to make a forced landing. As mentioned earlier, when the plane force-landed, the pilot lost his ability to use wireless communications. In such a situation, he would put a message that gave his location into the message cylinder on the pigeon's leg. Often the bird would have to fly through fog and strong headwinds over rough seas. One time a plane was forced to land five miles from land during strong winds and a thunderstorm. The pigeons on the plane made it back to the loft in an hour even when flying into the winds.

Unlike aircraft pilots, tank operators found pigeons indispensable because they had no other means of communication—they had no wireless capabilities and could not use human or dog runners.

The French valued their pigeons so much that they used about 30,000 during the Great War. Birds that performed exceptional service were awarded the Croix de Guerre or the Croix Militaire. They received diplomas that were kept at the headquarters of the French Pigeon Service and were given special bands to wear around their legs.

Cher Ami.

CHER AMI

One of the most famous pigeons used by the American army in World War I was Cher Ami. "Cher Ami [was] the black checker cock which delivered twelve important messages on the Verdun front and lost a leg in the Argonne. . . . The little courier was hit by a bullet just as he was leaving Grand Prè. The boys in the trenches saw him stagger and shouted, 'He's done for!' and watched to see where he would fall—but he didn't. For a few seconds he fluttered helplessly about, then gathering himself together he went on through the hail of shrapnel and machine-gun fire, and was out of sight. . . . Suddenly above his loft at Ramont he appears again, he drops from the sky like a rocket. Striking the loft, breast first, he staggers, sways from side to side, and then, hopping on one bloody leg, he makes for the entrance landing board . . . the tube bearing the message was hanging by the ligament of the leg that had been shot through; there was a hole through the breast bone made by the same bullet" (Baynes, *Animal Heroes of the Great War*, 116–117).

LORD ADELAIDE AND PRESIDENT WILSON

One of the more famous tank pigeons was Lord Adelaide, who made two successful runs, each time through a hail of bullets without being shot. On his third run he unfortunately was shot, but he still made it to his loft, even though he was bloody and weak. Another famous bird was President Wilson. He flew twelve and a half miles in twenty-one minutes with one leg shot away, and he did it through heavy rain and fog.

LE POILU

Often pigeons were kept in the trenches without proper shelter and time to rest. There are many stories of these amazing birds, but some stand out as spectacular. In one account, an important message about the location *Releasing a pigeon from a tank.* of an enemy ammunitions train had to be sent to the rear. This critical message was given to a bird named Le Poilu, who had an outstanding record. Le Poilu made it to his home base despite the fact that flesh and feathers hung from his neck in ribbons. He was so weak that he could not walk straight.

KAJA BOY, MOCKER, AND LADY JANE

Kaja Boy, also known as "the little streak," delivered his message despite being exhausted and wounded. Other successful pigeons were Mocker, who had one eye destroyed, and Lady Jane, who was gassed but still made it to her loft. According to the reports, these three birds recovered.

NO. 2709

A British bird known as No. 2709 served in the vicinity of Menin Road. On October 3, 1917, she was sent with a message in the afternoon to her loft nine miles away. When she did not return in a sufficient amount of time, she was given up for dead. However, it was later determined that she had been wounded and had spent the night in the rain. The next day she managed to return to her loft. She had been shot and had lost a leg, and the cylinder holding the message had been driven into her little body. She died before her trainer could read the message.

PILOT'S LUCK

A quite remarkable account is that of a pigeon known as Pilot's Luck. This particular bird was released from a seaplane 200 miles away from the pigeon's loft. The plane had engine trouble and had been attacked by the enemy. Pilot's Luck flew the 200 miles in five hours. On another occasion, Pilot's Luck and another bird were responsible for the rescue of a seaplane crew when they brought home the message for help. Another account has Pilot's Luck flying a message about fifty miles that resulted in the rescue of the crew.

RED COCK AKA CRISP, V.C.

Captain Crisp was in charge of the trawler Nelson when it was attacked by a German U-boat. Crisp fought well but was mortally wounded. Before he died, he sent Red Cock with a message for help. Red Cock flew to a nearby ship for assistance and therefore helped to save the surviving crew. For this action, Red Cock was renamed Crisp V.C. and was honored in the United Services Museum in Whitehall, London, England.

THE BLUE HEN

Although pigeons typically could fly about forty-five miles per hour, sometimes they did better than that. One account describes a blue hen that was released from a seaplane off of the Scottish coast on a cold, nasty November day. It was nearing dusk and the plane went down twenty-two miles from base. When the men were rescued, they learned that their little hen had flown twenty-two miles in about twenty-two minutes!

HOPE FOR THE PILOTS

Baynes (*Animal Heroes of the Great War*, 233–236) gives an excellent account of one incident that sums up the value and hope the pigeons gave to pilots.

It was late afternoon. One of England's largest seaplanes had just completed a long anti-submarine patrol above the North Sea, and her tired pilot gladly swung her around and headed for his base. Then something went wrong. The huge aircraft plunged downward, righted itself, plunged again, and dived sidewise into the water. There was an ominous cracking and ripping, some quick, dangerous work by the crew, and four men stood upon a wrecked and wave-swept seaplane. How long she would float, heavily laden as she was with motor and armament, none could tell, but what every man did know was that help must come quickly from somewhere, or it need not come at all.

Then someone shouted, "The pigeons!" A dripping basket was found and opened, but alas, two of the three birds were dead, and the survivor so wet and chilled that its recovery was doubtful. But it seemed the only chance, and an officer wrapped it in a woolen muffler which by some miracle was dry, and placed the bundle inside his shirt. In half an hour the pigeon had somewhat revived, and as the daylight was already falling, it was decided to wait no longer. A brief message was written, rolled up, and pushed into a small aluminum cylinder, and the cylinder attached to the right leg of the bird.

It was an anxious moment when the pilot climbed to a high point on the wreck and tossed the little messenger into the air. It fell, and every heart sank with it. Then, catching itself just above the waves, it lifted itself a little. For several seconds it barely held its own, then seeming to gain strength by its own effort, it rose slowly, squared away, and disappeared in the battleship grey.

Somewhere on the northeast coast of England night was approaching under a drizzly mist, and a raw wind whipped land and sea around the lonely group of buildings known as Royal Air Force Pigeon Station No. ... It was tea time, and a welcome hour to the little group of bronzed "non-coms" and men in the British uniform who were chatting and laughing around a small fire in the mess room. ... (the laughter stopped as they listened) ... to the sharp electric bell

55

that rings when a pigeon enters the "trap." A non-commissioned officer set down his cup of tea untasted, arose, and opened the door leading to the pigeon loft. From a corner where it had huddled, he lifted
a light blue pigeon, very wet and bedraggled, skillfully removed a
small aluminum cylinder from its right leg, slipped the bird into a
pigeon basket, and carried it into the mess room. . . .

Darkness had fallen on the North Sea, and four men, wet and
chilled, still clung to a wrecked seaplane. They had little hope that
their message had been delivered, or if it had been, that help would
come in time to save them. The wind had risen, and now and then the
waves tore some portion of the wreck, which sank lower and lower in
the water. At last there came a sound—the sweetest music they had
ever heard—the siren of a motorboat. Again and again it sounded,
each time nearer; then the heartened men arose and sent up a wild
shout in answer, and a hissing bow shot toward them from the darkness.

On top of a little basket by the fire in the mess room, a modest
blue pigeon sat quietly preening its damp feathers. And the next
morning the British papers reported, "Seaplane N 64 lost in the North
Sea, fifteen miles southeast of Rocky Point. *All the crew were saved.*"

An Airedale transporting pigeons.

An Airedale ready to transport pigeons.

SPIES, BALLOONISTS, AND AVIATORS NOT IN BATTLE

Spies also used pigeons as did balloonists and aviators who were not engaged in battle. The pigeons could be released from aircraft going 100 miles per hour and from heights of up to 6,000 feet. They would descend to their normal 300–500-foot range before flying to their lofts.

Pigeons in cages were dropped into enemy territory in hopes that loyal residents would send important information back to the troops in the message cylinders. This was such a threat to the Germans that residents risked severe punishment if they released any of the birds with messages.

Although pigeons were not used at night, two birds are credited for saving the lives of 1,500 Italians who were surrounded and for the capture of 3,500 Austrians when a message for help was sent with the birds at night.

Along with dogs, pigeons were an important means of communication. The main advantage to using pigeons was that they were easily transported and did not take up room.

As bird enthusiasts know, pigeons are very intelligent and capable of being trained. One can only appreciate the loyalty and steadfastness of these little birds when you consider that birds instinctively shy away from danger. Yet the pigeons flew through gun fire, bombs, gas and in some cases severe weather. Sometimes the birds were near death from the cold and being wet, yet when warmed and partly dried, they flew home to deliver their messages.

CHAPTER 5

THE MASCOTS

THE THERAPEUTIC VALUE OF MASCOTS

The rules about keeping pets and mascots in the military during World War I were much more forgiving than they are today. Every war has had its share of mascots that were either openly kept by soldiers and sailors or smuggled and hidden from the authorities. Today we realize that these mascots and pets provided therapeutic value in situations where it was desperately needed. In peacetime these animals still provide therapeutic services.

During World War I, many of the mascots were not taken with the soldiers to the front, but they served to ease tensions and entertain the soldiers while they waited to be deployed. Many soldiers either brought their pets with them or adopted one while in battle or between campaigns. Although these mascots did not have formal training, some of the canine mascots served in the same capacity as well-trained war dogs; they just seemed to know what to do.

Almost every imaginable animal became a mascot. And today we would be amazed at how they behaved. One officer in the Balkans had a golden eagle as a pet. He had raised the bird from when it was a baby chick. The bird was tame and would even allow other people to pet him. The bird was permitted to fly free each day for exercise and would always return to his owner (Baynes, *Animal Heroes of the Great War*, 3).

The mascots often represented a symbol of home for the troops. For example, a group from Australia had a kangaroo as a mascot. An English battalion that had served in India had an Indian antelope. Various South African troops adopted a parrot, a gazelle, and monkeys. The Americans had coyotes, raccoons, and eagles.

Golden eagle as a mascot.

Goat mascot.

Some of the Canadian regiments had black bears as mascots. The Welsh often had a goat as a mascot, and it was usually named Taffy after an old nursery rhyme.

Most of the mascots did not go into battle with the soldiers due to the impracticality of taking them along. They were kept at the camps in England while the soldiers waited to be sent to France. On the other hand, many of the more practical mascots, such as dogs, cats, and goats, were taken to the camps in France, and some even went into the trenches with their masters.

PRINCE THE IRISH TERRIER

A common story at the time of the Great War was about dogs running away from home and finding their masters in the trenches. Most of these accounts were fiction or wishful thinking. However, one account has been verified as true.

In his book *Animal War Heroes*, Peter Shaw Baker gives a detailed account of Prince and verifies that the dog did find his way to France. It seems that when Mr. Brown left for France, Prince was distraught and would not be consoled. One day when he was let out by Mr. Brown's wife, he did not come back. It remains a mystery how Prince found his way to his master's trench in France.

The news about Prince's remarkable feat spread, and Private Brown was asked to go before the commanding officer to verify the exploit. Prince was adopted as the regiment's mascot and stayed with the men for the entire war. The soldiers made a vest for Prince, and when Private Brown was awarded the

Ambulance dogs in the trenches.

1914–15 Star Medal, the Victory Medal, and the British War Medal, they were pinned on Prince's vest.

The soldiers taught Prince many tricks, and he was a constant source of amusement and comfort to them. He could balance a penny on his nose, and, on command, he would run around looking for any pair of legs that were not clad in a khaki uniform. If he found non-khaki legs, he would grab the pants leg and tug.

Prince also learned how to survive in war conditions by hiding when he heard incoming heavy shells.

Prince followed Private Brown's friend, Weaver, when he took his horse up the line to distribute food. He would sit on the horse's saddle with the reins in his mouth. However, Prince earned his keep many times over by killing the rats in the trenches. It is recorded that he killed 137 rats in one day.

Much to everyone's deep sorrow, Prince disappeared one day. It was very upsetting to the soldiers to think that Prince may have been killed, which was always a risk in the trenches. However, a message came from another unit ten miles away that Prince was with them. It seems that they had a terrier bitch that was in heat.

Prince survived the war and returned to England. Because Private Brown could not afford the cost of the six-month quarantine that was required by England, the Royal Society for the Prevention of Cruelty to Animals came to the rescue. (The RSPCA was instrumental in helping war animals meet England's quarantine requirements.)

Prince was so popular and well known that, until his death, people would send him cards and visit him. One Scotsman even sent him a Christmas cake (Baynes, *Animal Heroes of the Great War*, 7; Baker, *Animal War Heroes*, 1–5).

FIGHTING MAC THE RETRIEVER MIX

Sergeant-Major Mac was sort of a Christmas puppy. His owner, Sergeant-Major Balcombe, was attached to the 449th Siege Battery, Royal Garrison Artillery. The battery was in the Battle at the Somme front, near Gouzeaucourt Wood, in the fall of 1917.

Balcombe was sent to a nearby town to get some poultry or whatever he could find to add to the men's diet, because it was close to Christmas. As he was walking through the marketplace, he heard puppies crying and went to check it out. He found a basket with puppies and an old French peasant trying to sell them. The peasant tried to convince Balcombe that the puppies were English Collies resulting from the mating of French army dogs. As it turned out, the puppies were three parts retriever.

Being a dog lover, Balcombe could not resist paying twenty francs for a puppy. When he returned, he had the six-week-old puppy tucked inside the pocket of his coat to protect it from the snow and cold. No mention is made whether or not he got the Christmas poultry!

One of his comrades, a Scotsman, claimed that he could see strength and a bold attitude in the pup and named him Fighting Mac after Sir Hector Archibald MacDonald, one of the few British soldiers to earn the rank of general on his own merit by working up through the ranks. He was highly respected by the soldiers.

Mac had his first taste of war at about seven weeks of age when he was following his mas-

Messenger war dog and soldier with gas masks.

ter across a field and a German shell burst near him. Poor Mac was thrown and buried by debris. Not surprisingly, he was frightened for a few weeks but quickly got over it. He would even stay in the battery lines close to the guns, but he did learn to dig a trench and take cover in it when the bombing started.

One time, he was gassed and wounded at the same time his master was knocked unconscious. Mac stayed with his master and barked for someone to come.

Another day, as the war progressed, a German airplane dropped a bomb that threw Mac quite a distance. After that, whenever he heard the sound of a German plane approaching, he would lie down very flat on the ground, look skyward, and snarl. On more than one occasion, Mac was able to alert the soldiers when they could not hear a plane approaching because they were operating heavy equipment. The soldiers learned to watch Mac as an early warning sign of an air attack.

During a hasty retreat of about seventy-five miles, Mac panicked and started to run toward the enemy lines. Like any dog that runs in a panic, no amount of calling or whistling got his attention. It was if he could not hear the calls.

His master and the soldiers who loved him mourned because they believed that Mac was dead. They could not imagine how he could have survived such a massive retreat of men, machines, and horses. Yet four days later, Mac showed up, very thin and totally exhausted. Needless to say, there were a lot of happy soldiers.

After the war was over, Balcombe was ordered to Germany with the Army of Occupation; however, dogs were not allowed. After much soul searching, Balcombe decided that he would have Mac put to sleep rather than leave him with strangers. They were sitting in the animal hospital, Mac in Balcombe's arms, as the veterinarian was just about to give Mac the lethal injection, when a runner rushed up with a pass for Mac.

Balcombe and Mac stayed together for the rest of Balcombe's tour. When Balcombe was discharged from the army, Mac was shipped to England with the help of Our Dumb Friends' League and lived the rest of his life with Balcombe. However, to his dying day, every time he heard an airplane approaching, he would lie down and snarl. Mac died at the age of nine and was mourned deeply.

Balcombe is recorded as saying that he valued Mac's friendship the most when he was in the army. He explained that Mac comforted him in his darkest hours.

CRUMP THE GRIFFON MIX

A rather comical mascot was a little Griffon mixed breed named Crump. He was given as a gift to General Sir E. Stuart Wortley, CB, CMG. Whenever the general rode his horse, the soldiers could see little Crump sitting on the saddle in front. Crump had a fondness for cigarettes and pipes and would often walk with a lit cigarette in a holder or his pipe between his teeth. He was certainly the source of amusement for anyone who saw him.

Crump.

TOMMY THE GERMAN SHEPHERD DOG

Another famous mascot was a German Shepherd dog (known as an Alsatian at the time) named Tommy, who became a fixture at the Paris branch of the American Red Cross after the war. He proudly wore the Croix de Guerre medal (the Cross of War, usually given to foreign military forces that were French allies who distinguished themselves in battle) as perhaps the mascot who had seen the most fighting of all.

Tommy started his war career as a German mascot but, at the Battle of Amiens in 1915, he was captured with a group of German soldiers by Canadian Scots. Tommy seemed to enjoy living with the Scottish regiment and stayed with them until the end of the war. Even though he had his own gas mask, he was gassed badly once during battle but recovered fully.

Tommy was an inspiration to the men, because he often led an attack and always went "over the top" (over the top of the trench) with the men. During his years in battle, he was "owned" by fifteen different officers, because each was either killed or wounded. When the Scottish regiment was awarded the Croix de Guerre for their bravery in battle, without exception, all of the soldiers voted to give it to Tommy.

FEND L'AIR THE SETTER

One of the most famous mascots was owned by a sergeant in the French army. Fend l'Air was a black and white setter who managed to get on board his owner's ship, landed at Marseilles, and crossed France into Belgium. He stayed by his owner's side throughout the battles, including the victory at the Marne. But one night a shell exploded in their trench and buried the sergeant alive.

Fend l'Air, who was unhurt, searched for and found where his owner was buried

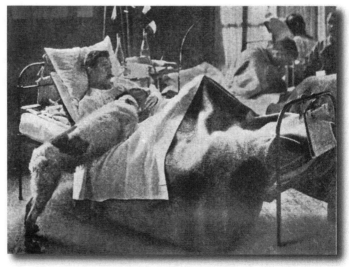

The sergeant and Fend l'Air.

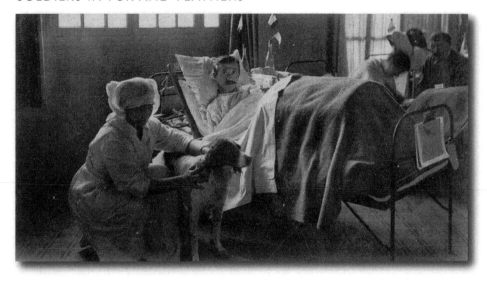

alive but unconscious and dug his master's head out of the dirt and rocks. Then he barked nonstop for three days until his master was rescued. When the ambulance took the sergeant away, Fend l'Air followed close behind even though he was exhausted and had bloody paws.

At first, Fend l'Air was shooed away from the field hospital, but when the head nurse heard what happened, she set up a cot next to the sergeant for Fend l'Aire. The first thing that the sergeant saw and felt when he regained consciousness was his beloved Fend l'Air.

A PILOT'S MASCOT

Pilots also had mascots, and one pilot tells of adopting a small unwanted dog from French peasants. The pilot tells how brokenhearted the dog was at being left behind, and so the

Pilots' mascots.

pilot would let the dog curl up by his feet during flights. The dog never moved while they were in flight. When the dog was left alone with the airplane, he guarded it so well that no one could approach it.

SPOT THE FOX TERRIER

General Townshend had a Fox Terrier named Spot as a mascot. Townshend led his infantry force, the 6th Poona Division, in a campaign in the Middle East near Baghdad. However, he was eventually defeated by the Germans and Turks led by Nur-Ud-Din and Baron von der Goltz. Because Townshend was able to hold the city of Kut el Amara for a number of months before his defeat, Spot earned the nickname of Spot o' Kut.

When the British were captured, the men were treated cruelly and many died; however, General Townshend was respected and treated with honor. Spot was also captured but was allowed to stay with Townshend until the general was sent to Constantinople. Because it was against Turkish law for the general to take his dog with him, Spot was sent down the Tigris River under a white flag of truce and given to the British forces. From there he was sent back to England and stayed with a friend of General Townshend.

VERDUN BELLE THE SETTER

Another famous mascot was a setter bitch named Verdun Belle, who wandered into an American regiment in France. She was starving and caked with mud. A young marine decided to adopt her and gave her food and a bath. They became a devoted pair, with Belle always sleeping at her master's side and quietly following him into battle. Once she was gassed, and after that her master fashioned a gas mask for her. Whenever the Germans started a gas attack, Belle would run to retrieve her gas mask so that the marine could put it on her face.

All went well until the following spring when Belle gave birth to seven puppies. Just as the puppies were born, the regiment received orders to travel across France to help halt the Germans at Marne. At first the soldier took the puppies in an old wicker-shell basket that he carried along with all of his gear. Along the way, all but two of the puppies died, and the soldier put the remaining puppies in his shirt.

At one point the regiment had to pass through a town that was packed with refugees and soldiers. Verdun Belle was lost in the confusion, and the soldier found himself with two hungry puppies to feed.

The marine begged some milk from a farmer and fed the puppies from an eyedropper. However, as he neared the front, he realized that he could not keep the motherless puppies and gave them to soldiers who remained at the farm. The story does not end there, however.

The next morning, while Verdun Belle followed another regiment of marines, they passed by the hospital on the farm. She suddenly stopped, sniffed the air, and ran to a tree in the field. There in a bundle of bloody bandages

Unnamed mascot.

Dog and soldier with gas masks.

near the hospital were her two puppies, sound asleep. Belle was allowed to stay with her pups on the farm.

Sometime later, as wounded men were brought from the front to the hospital, Verdun Belle went crazy with excitement. It was her master, shell shocked and unconscious. As the young marine regained consciousness, he felt Belle's soft tongue licking the dirt off of his face. As he recovered on a cot in the shade of a tree, Verdun Belle lay in her own cot next to him, nursing two puppies.

RAGS AND TATTERS THE SEALYHAM MIXES

Rags and Tatters were two mixed-breed Sealyham Terrier puppies born in the trenches of France in 1917. They stayed with the soldiers for at least a year and did a stellar job of keeping the trenches rat and rodent free. (There is no record of what became of Tatters.)

After the war, the soldier who owned Rags wanted to send her home but could not due to the cost of the quarantine and other expenses involved in shipping her home. While Rags was in quarantine, the soldier wrote to the secretary of the Royal Society for the Prevention of Cruelty to Animals, Captain

Fairholme, asking that if a home could not be found for Rags, to put her to sleep. When Captain Fairholme saw Rags, he adopted her himself.

It did not take Rags long to endear herself to the entire household. She had a few rather amusing traits that would make the family laugh. Although Rags had been well trained by the soldiers and was a delight to have around, if she did not like the direction her owner headed on a walk, she would throw herself down, roll over on her back, and stick her four feet in the air. If that did not work, she would act as if she was too weak to walk and would have to be dragged along.

It is reported that one day she was in a room in the house and became cold because the weather was chilly. She carried on and barked until someone came to see what she was barking about. As soon as the person came into the room, she ran between the door and the gas fireplace until they lit it. Once the room was warm, she settled down.

Rags lived a long, happy life and died at the ripe old age of thirteen in 1930.

OLD BILL THE WIRE-HAIRED FOX TERRIER

The navy also had mascots but not nearly as many as the army. One unusual incident occurred when the HMS *Falmouth* attacked and sank five German trawlers. These boats were sometimes made of wood and could be difficult to sink. They had to be sunk to keep the boating lanes clear and safe for other ships. However, one of the trawlers would not sink. The British shelled the trawler numerous times, but the ship, even filled with water, would not sink. Finally they rammed the trawler and cut it in half.

Old Bill.

One can only imagine their shock when they examined the remains of the ship and saw, sitting on one-half, a small Fox Terrier, wagging its tail! The sailors of the *Falmouth* rescued the little dog. However, they saw a collar on the dog with the name of Fritz, which was unacceptable, and they all refused to go into battle until the name was changed. Fritz therefore became Fred, and later his name was changed to Old Bill.

Old Bill had a number of close calls while he was on the *Falmouth*. Just a few weeks after he was rescued, he was on deck with one of the sailors during a particularly bad storm when both the sailor and Old Bill were thrown across the deck of the ship. The sailor's elbows caught in the scuppers (the drain holes in the low wall on the deck) and prevented him from going overboard. Old Bill's front paws landed on the sailor's chest, saving the dog as well. The ship lurched again and they both were thrown to safety.

Later the *Falmouth* was torpedoed by a German U-boat. She did not sink at that time and was slowly heading to port, escorted by two destroyers, when she was torpedoed again and sank. All of the crew as well as Old Bill were rescued.

After living through so many close calls, Old Bill was sent to the Plymouth Barracks, where he remained a mascot and lived to an old age.

DICKYBUSH THE WIRE-HAIRED FOX TERRIER

Dickybush's life almost literally started with a bang. Major Melvin Hall, DSO, found a terribly frightened female terrier at a place called Dickebusch (Belgium), a few miles from Ypres. She was starving and almost out of her mind with fear. Hall decided to take her and nurse her back to health. Not long after that she gave birth to a litter of puppies, Dickybush being one of them.

During an attack on the town where Hall was stationed, an enemy plane dropped a bomb on the house where he was assigned to work. The terrier bitch was sleeping at his feet at the time and her litter in a basket nearby in a corner of the room.

When the bomb exploded, several staff members were killed or wounded, and all of the dogs, except for Dickybush, were killed. Luckily, Hall was not injured. Dickybush was only a few days old at this time; his eyes were not even open yet.

Hall raised Dickybush, who was his constant companion throughout the war. They both survived, and Dickybush lived a long, happy life, although for the remainder of his days, he did not like gunfire.

PEGGY AND JUMBO THE OLD ENGLISH BULLDOGS

In some cases, people would donate their pet as a mascot with the understanding that the pet would be returned after the war. One such case was an English Bulldog named Peggy. She was just a puppy when her owner donated her to the crew of the HMS *Iron Duke*. She was in a number of battles, including the famous Battle of Jutland (Denmark). The battle lasted for two days and was a

Peggy.

huge effort by the British Royal Navy's Grand Fleet. It included ships and personnel from the Royal Australian Navy and the Royal Canadian Navy, fighting
against the Imperial German Navy's High Seas Fleet (May 31 and June 1, 1916).

Later, the Royal Navy had a medal made for Peggy commemorating the
battle. She also wore the General Service and Victory ribbons.

Peggy was not the only dog on the ship. She had a companion named
Jumbo who was also an English Bulldog; however, he was left at base when the
ship went to sea because he always got seasick. Jumbo and Peggy had a litter of
five pups during the war.

Peggy was known for her pranks and tricks and would pick up anything
that was left on deck—hats, shoes, socks—and hide them in her kennel. She
also had a sport that had the sailors rolling in laughter. Every morning the
sailors would gather for prayer, and right after prayers, the band would play as
the sailors jogged around the deck. Peggy would hide under one of the gun tur-
rets, and when the mood struck her, she would rush out, grab a sailor by the
pant leg, knock him over, and then run and hide under a turret to wait for her
next victim.

She also loved sports, and when the men played soccer, she would always be there. If the onlookers were not happy with the game, they would shout, "Give it to Peggy! Give it to Peggy!" When she heard this she would rush in and join the game.

After the war, she was returned to her owner as promised despite the crew's efforts—which included begging, pleading, and offering to buy her—to keep her.

Peggy spent the next few years raising money for St. Bartholomew's Hospital until, in 1920, she was given back to the *Iron Duke* because it had become obvious that that was where Peggy wanted to be. Every time she saw a sailor, she would become excited and greet him as a long-lost friend.

The Royal Navy sent a destroyer on a special trip just to bring Peggy back to the *Iron Duke*, which was out at sea. Needless to say, the sailors were overjoyed.

YEL THE MIXED BREED

Another naval mascot was a dog named Yel, whose full name was Yelverstone. He was a rather large, heavy-coated dog from Dartmoor and was owned by Commander Davenport. Yel spent time on shore as well as on a ship. He went to South Africa, where he encountered some mishaps. Davenport had a colored servant, named Snowball, who became devoted to Yel. While on shore, Snowball protected Yel from natives who might have enjoyed him for dinner. He meticulously groomed Yel and removed ticks and fleas from him daily.

Once when Yel stumbled on a black ant nest, it was Snowball's quick action that saved Yel from being infested and bitten by the ants. Snowball was able to get Yel to a nearby pond, where Snowball dunked him. Yel returned the loyalty by saving Snowball from two poisonous snakes that were hidden in the brush.

Commander Davenport was hunting a leopard one day, and Yel was leading the pursuit. The leopard turned and leaped at Yel, who would have been killed had it not been for the quick response of Davenport, who shot the leopard. As it turned out, the leopard had two cubs, which the men took. Ironically, the cubs stayed with Yel in his kennel for awhile.

Yel disliked gunfire and made the association that, when he heard a submarine, it usually meant gunfire. With his keen sense of hearing, Yel could detect the approach of a submarine before anyone else. The sailors learned that, when Yel became upset, it meant that a submarine was approaching; conversely, if Yel was calm, they were safe.

After the war, Yel returned to Dartmoor with Commander Davenport to live a long, peaceful life.

British war dog with coat and gas mask.

RAGS THE OLD ENGLISH SHEEPDOG MIX

Rags was a common name for a shaggy type of dog. One such Rags was a mixed-breed Old English Sheepdog that the Lancashire Fusiliers adopted when he was a puppy. When the unit landed on V Beach at Gallipoli, Rags wandered off. It was a common practice during wartime to put stray dogs to sleep, but Rags was spared when Midshipman Forbes adopted him. Forbes was assigned to the HMS *Cornwallis* off of Gallipoli.

Rags stayed with the midshipman throughout the war and served on a number of ships while traveling widely. He escaped death at least three times, even when the ship he was on struck a floating mine and was sunk. Fortunately, all hands were saved, including Rags.

When Forbes was awarded the Distinguished Service Cross after the war, he took Rags with him to Buckingham Palace.

Rags spent the rest of his life with Forbes. Rags had a favorite peacetime sport, which was to chase rocks that were thrown into the water—the bigger the better. Once he retrieved a rock that weighed fourteen pounds. He apparently liked to hear the rocks splash in the water.

BRUCE THE SCOTTISH TERRIER AND LASSIE THE COLLIE

True to the glorified naval tradition that a ship's captain should go down with his ship, Captain Loxley was seen on the bridge of the ill-fated battleship *Formidable*, a cigarette between his lips and his Scottish Terrier Bruce at his side, ready to start their final journey together.

However, some sailors were rescued from the *Formidable*, and one unconscious sailor named John Cowan was left for dead after all efforts to revive him failed. His body was left on the kitchen floor of the Pilot Boat Hotel while the medics took care of the sailors who were still alive. The resident dog, a cross-bred, rough-coated Collie named Lassie, walked into the kitchen unnoticed. Lassie went over to Cowan and started to lick his face while she lay next to him. She would not stop, but because everyone was so busy, they did not pay much attention to her. However, after half an hour, Cowan started to moan lowly and move his hands and legs. Thanks to Lassie, he was taken care of and went on to survive.

RIN-TIN-TIN THE ALSATIAN

Perhaps the most famous mascot was Rin-Tin-Tin. He was born in a German trench in Metz. When the Germans retreated, Rin-Tin-Tin was deserted by his mother; however, Lieutenant Lee-Duncan found him in a dugout, nursed him, and kept him alive.

At the end of the war, Duncan took Rin-Tin-Tin back to America. And, because Duncan was a police-dog trainer, Rin-Tin-Tin was trained for police work. Duncan entered him in the Police Dog Trials, which were being filmed. When Duncan saw Rin-Tin-Tin on film, he recognized the dog's potential for working in the film industry.

It did not take long for Duncan to have a contract and work for Rin-Tin-Tin. It is said that Rin-Tin-Tin was very smart and learned the tricks he had to perform quickly. Duncan did not allow people to make a fuss over the dog, who seemed to get his reward by doing his job.

Rin-Tin-Tin started his career in silent movies, which were easy for him because he could be directed by voice commands from Duncan, who would stand out of camera range while giving the commands.

Once movies became "talkies," Duncan had to find a way to signal Rin-Tin-Tin. He found the solution with some of Rin-Tin-Tin's toys. When Rinty was shown a black velvet cat, he would go into a mad fury. A stuffed lion made him bark, and a little woolen rabbit made him wag his tail.

Rin-Tin-Tin lived to the age of fourteen and was buried with his toys in Santa Monica.

UNNAMED CANINE MASCOT

A number of accounts describe soldiers risking their lives and being killed in their efforts to save a mascot on the front lines. One story is about Midshipman Sydney T. Warr-Buckler, who, during a gale, with the ship covered in ice, dove into the sea to save the ship's canine mascot who had fallen overboard. Despite his heavy clothing, rough seas, and the extreme cold, he managed to save the dog, swim to a rope thrown overboard, and save himself and the dog. The Royal Society for the Prevention of Cruelty to Animals awarded him a silver medal for his gallantry.

JANE AND JIMMY—GOOSE AND GANDER

Jane and Jimmy were the mascots of A Battery, 52nd Brigade, RFA, for almost five years. Jimmy and Jane were lucky that one of the soldiers took a special fancy to them, because they were purchased in December 1915 to be fattened for Christmas dinner.

Because some of the soldiers were looking forward to a Christmas goose dinner, they decided to hold a "trial" to determine the fate of the geese. The jury decided that the birds were too cute to eat, and thus began their career as the brigade's mascots.

The birds traveled most of the time with Gunner Grey in the mess cart. They were a comical sight with their heads hanging out of the sides of the mess cart, much to the amusement of the soldiers.

At one point during a battle, both Jane and Jimmy were stolen by a Belgian farmer. Because the soldiers were under heavy fire, they assumed that Jimmy and Jane had been killed. However, the next morning they were found very much alive in the farmer's yard. The farmer refused to say how they got there and the soldiers regained their mascots.

Both Jimmy and Jane stayed with their soldiers until the end of the war. They were taken to the London Zoo after a bit of a delay over whether or not they should be quarantined.

JIMMY THE DONKEY

Jimmy was born in the trenches, and, when he was only a few weeks old, his mother, who was actually captured from the Germans, was killed in action. Jimmy was adopted by the 1st Battalion, The Cameronians as their mascot (Peter

Shaw Baker, *Animal War Heroes*, 62).

The soldiers doted on him. They fed him canned milk and taught him to do tricks such as standing up on his hind legs to beg for biscuits and jam. He would also put his forelegs around a soldier's neck and give him a kiss, or he would stand at the entrance of a trench and lift a foreleg to "shake hands."

Although he was wounded seven times by shrapnel (but never seriously), Jimmy stayed with his battalion until the end of the war.

Jimmy helped out by carrying handgun ammunition and other supplies to the firing line. In one incident, as Jimmy was carrying supplies, an airplane crashed near him. The pilot was not seriously wounded but was shaken. When he saw Jimmy, he also saw the flasks of whiskey in the pannier on his back. Needless to say, the whiskey helped to calm his nerves.

Jimmy.

After the war, Jimmy was sent with other draft animals to the Remount Depot to be sold. Because of the tricks he had learned, some circus people wanted to buy him. However, Mrs. Heath, the secretary of the Royal Society for the Prevention of Cruelty to Animals, felt that Jimmy deserved a better home. She raised enough money to buy Jimmy and was able to purchase him.

Because of his war wounds, Heath decided to have Jimmy X-rayed in case some shrapnel remained in his body. Jimmy wanted no part of being X-rayed, but after a contest of wills, the X-rays were done. Fortunately, no shrapnel was detected.

Jimmy never forgot his soldier buddies, because one day when he was on a fund-raising mission for the RSPCA, one of his former buddies happened to see Jimmy and went over to him. Jimmy instantly recognized the man, put his forelegs around the man's neck, and gave him a kiss.

A French mascot.

ROYAL SOCIETY FOR THE PREVENTION OF CRUELTY TO ANIMALS

It is fitting to mention that the RSPCA set up a hospital/boarding facility to house the animals that served in World War I with their masters. Many were mascots, and most of the soldiers could not afford to pay for their companions to spend the six-month quarantine required to enter England. The RSPCA provided this for the soldiers, who, at the end of the six months, for a small fee, could be reunited with their animal companions.

Besides the R.S.P.C.A., other humane organizations contributed veterinary services during and after the war. The Blue Cross, a veterinary branch of the Dumb Friends League of England set up hospitals throughout the war zones. The United States sent representatives from the American Veterinary Medical Association and The Amerian Humane Society to assist with the care and treatment of all of the animals that served in World War I. The American Red Cross also assisted in every way they could and functioned as a focal point for smaller volunteer groups who wanted to contribute to the war effort. The American Red Star Animal Relief organization was established to help raise money and supplies for the animals serving in World War I. (Baynes, *Animal Heroes of the Great War*, 282-294).

PRINNY THE ITALIAN GREYHOUND

One of the more famous dogs to stay at the RSPCA home was an Italian Greyhound named Prinny, who was owned by an officer and had seen many battles. This was determined by the engraving on his collar: "Gaza, Beersheba, Jaffa, Jerusalem, Jericho, Torpedoed 27-5-18. HMT *Leastowe Castle*" (Baynes, *Animal Heroes of the Great War*, 18).

Other information about Prinny is scarce, but he is typical of dogs that spent a long time at war and lived through many battles. Prinny was especially regal in his attitude and helped raise money for the RSPCA.

JACK—NURSE CAVELL'S DOG

The RSPCA used some of the animals to raise money to pay for their efforts. The most famous dog was Jack, who was owned by an English nurse, Miss Edith Cavell. Nurse Cavell owned Jack for ten years before she was killed by the Germans in Belgium. Jack mourned the death of his mistress and his health suffered as a result.

For various reasons, no one wanted Jack, and he became neglected and thin. Dowager Duchess de Croy took Jack in and nursed him back to health. She would sometimes take him to exhibits, one of which was a dog show at Lille, where people took more than a thousand photos of him for the benefit of the French Red Cross. Jack lived to a ripe old age of about sixteen years and died on February 16, 1923.

SERGEANT STUBBY

Stubby was a stray dog that wandered around Yale and was adopted by John Robert Conway, who was in training for the war. Stubby became a popular figure by learning the bugle calls and marching with the soldiers.

He was hidden on the transport ship in a coal bin but was soon discovered and became the mascot of the 102nd Infantry, 26th Yankee Division.

When the troops landed in France, he went into battle with them. As other mascots have done, Stubby learned to warn the soldiers of incoming bombs. He was also useful in finding wounded men.

In one encounter, he found a German spy who was sneaking around near the trenches and attacked him by grabbing the man by the seat of his pants and refusing to let go. He was thereafter given the rank of sergeant.

Stubby was given various medals for his activities in the war. He was made a lifetime member of the Red Cross, the YMCA, and the American Legion.

Sergeant Stubby.

He also met three presidents—Wilson, Harding, and Coolidge. He remained Conroy's companion until his death.

Stubby's remains and the coat he wore with all of his medals are on display in the Smithsonian Museum.

PITOUTCHI THE CAT

It is hard to imagine that a cat in the trenches could save a man's life, but that is exactly what Pitoutchi did. In the Belgian military records is the following recommendation: "Pitoutchi, 3rd Regiment of Artillery, for showing great bravery under fire, rare endurance, and remarkable initiative. Showed proof, in the course of a campaign, of the finest military qualities. Seeing his captain in danger, did not hesitate to expose himself in his place, courageously drawing upon himself the enemy fire, and foiling the maneuvers of the adversary by making them mistake the above-mentioned officer for a cat. At the front since his birth" (Baker, *Animal War Heroes*, 69).

Pitoutchi was born in the Belgian trenches. His mother was killed before the litter of eight kittens had opened their eyes. Lieutenant Lekeux was on duty when he heard the kittens crying and found a group of soldiers around a small basket of kittens. He decided to take them and nurse them. He tried the best he could to put drops of milk into their mouths, but the kittens would not drink it. By the next evening, all but one kitten had died. Only the little white kitten would drink the milk, and he survived. Although Pitoutchi survived, he never grew very big; he was, however, noted for his keen intelligence.

Kitten mascot.

Pitoutchi was devoted to Lekeux and followed him wherever he went. If the ground was dry, he would walk with Lekeux in the trenches. If the ground was wet, he would jump onto Lekeux's shoulder and ride.

The incident about which Lekeux wrote the report happened as follows.

The Germans were up to something for a number of days, throwing dirt near a thicket. Lekeux was concerned and decided to investigate what was going on, so with Pitoutchi on his shoulder, he left the trenches to investigate.

As Lekeux reached a spot near the German lines, he saw that they were digging a new trench. He hid himself in a shell hole near-by to make a sketch of the German works. He was so absorbed in his sketch that he did not notice three approaching German soldiers on patrol. When he finally realized his situation, it was too late to run. If he left the hole he would be shot, and if he stayed he would be bayo-neted, because it was obvious that the Germans had seen him crawl into the shell hole.

He decided to lie very still, hoping that the Germans would not see him, but unfortunately he heard one soldier say, "He's in the hole," so he knew he had been seen.

When Pitoutchi heard the German say that, he jumped out of the hole onto a piece of timber. The Germans were startled and fired two shots at Pitoutchi. However, as frightened as he was, Pitoutchi was not hit, and he jumped back into the hole with his beloved Lekeux.

The Germans laughed and joked that they had mistaken a cat for a man and left. Lekeux finished his drawings and returned to the Belgian lines with Pitoutchi on his shoulder.

JIMMY THE CAT

No one knows about the first four or five years of Jimmy's life. He was a beautiful lemon and white cat who made it from the trenches to Victoria Station in London, England, with his wounded owner, an Australian who was on his way to the hospital.

As fate would have it, Mr. F. Conway, who was a cook in the navy, was at Victoria Station to meet some friends. When Conway saw Jimmy, he struck up a conversation with the soldier. When he learned that the soldier could not take Jimmy with him, he offered to adopt Jimmy.

After his leave, Conway was assigned to the HMS *King George* and took Jimmy with him.

The HMS *King George* was part of the Grand Fleet and the flagship for Vice-Admiral Sr. M. Jerram. Soon after departure, they met the enemy and the guns started blasting. Jimmy was on deck and was wounded by shrapnel on his left ear. Conway was surprised that Jimmy did not seem to mind the noise of the guns. It took several weeks of care for his wound to heal, but once it did, Jimmy was once again on deck.

After that tour, Conway was reassigned to the HMS *Renown* and, of course, Jimmy went him. As it turned out, Jimmy was the only mascot on board the *Renown* and the crew fell in love with him. Jimmy mingled with the crew and was usually on hand when they engaged in sports. He was always ready for petting and socializing, but each night, Jimmy slept with Conway. It is almost comical that every morning, Jimmy would wake Conway up at exactly 6 A.M. by tapping him on the face with his paw.

Because Conway was a cook, Jimmy used to sit on a shelf in the galley and watch Conway work. If a piece of food was put aside (sometimes on purpose), Jimmy would push it with his paw and knock it to the floor, where he would enjoy the snack.

Jimmy's sea adventures ended when Conway came home on leave in 1917. Because Jimmy's ear was acting up again, Conway decided to leave him in the care of Our Dumb Friends League Cat's Home at Chelsea.

Mrs. Brockwell, the secretary of the home, adopted Jimmy and used to take him on fund-raising excursions. He was often visited by his old shipmates and lived to an old age. Because he became quite a celebrity, many people mourned his death in 1924.

The entertainment and companionship that the mascots gave the soldiers is evident by the fact that their stories have been preserved. The deep love that the soldiers and general public had for these mascots is illustrated by their success in raising money for various causes and the care they received after the war. What may be difficult to understand today is that these animals were often a major source of entertainment for the soldiers. They provided a brief respite from the war and a connection to home at a time when there was no television, radio, or phone contact with loved ones at home, even letters were infrequent.

Caring for a mascot gave the soldier something to think about other than the war. Playing with and sleeping with a mascot provided a sense of security for many soldiers. It is amazing to read about those mascots who without training knew what to do to save a soldier from certain death. Often, a canine mascot provided the important service of keeping an area free of rats and other rodents that were a constant problem. The rodents spread disease, ate food and would sometimes bite soldiers. Mascots are the unsung heroes of the Great War.

CHAPTER 6

HORSES AND MULES

TRANSPORT

Even though World War I was a mechanized war, horses and mules were invaluable. The motor vehicles of the Great War could not travel in deep mud, through water such as rivers, up steep banks, or through shell-pitted fields.

Dead transport war horses.

Artillery horses in battle.

The United States was a primary source of mules and horses for the Allies and shipped two-thirds of the animals, if not more. It is estimated that more than sixteen million mules and horses served with the Allies in World War I. Many of these animals are credited with saving the lives of the soldiers beside whom they fought.

It was common for a supply company to move heavy equipment up long, steep hills covered in slippery, sticky mud and littered with shell holes. The horses and mules were weak and tired because there was little time for them to rest to fully recuperate from the previous day's work. A horse or mule needs solid ground on which to stand in order to sleep or rest properly; however, war conditions were mostly filled with mud. The animals had to spend most of their rest time lifting one foot after another in order to keep from sinking into the mud.

PAIR OF BAY HORSES

A team of Missouri mules was struggling to haul a rolling kitchen up a mud-caked hill when they reached a shell hole and could not—would not—go further. Mule handlers say that a mule is smarter than a horse and will not try to haul what is beyond his ability to do so.

Nothing would get these mules to go any further. In the column was a pair of Thoroughbred-mix bay horses. The soldier, who was assigned to the two horses, worshipped the horses and had taken very good care of them. As a result, the horses were in the best shape that the situation would allow. As a pair, the horses had a lot of heart, which was evident by the way in which they pawed the mud,

84

anxious to move on. Unfortunately, the soldier in charge of moving the equipment noticed this and ordered the pair to be brought up to the mules and hitched in front of them to pull the load out of the shell hole.

The horses did this with such heart that they were ordered to help repeatedly. Even though they reached the point where they shook and trembled in their harnesses, they never gave up. Unfortunately, that night the game little bays did die in their harnesses. Their handler was inconsolable.

It is hard to imagine the conditions that these animals had to endure. The shell holes in the roads were often so deep and filled with water that men and animals drowned in them.

Transport war horses in the Battle at the Somme.

Once a horse or mule fell into a hole, it almost always meant death, often from a bullet to put the animal out of its misery. Even if a wagon or animal got near the edge of the hole, the mud was so soft and slippery that the wagon or animal would slip into the hole. As hard as the soldiers tried to save the animal, often they could not. Keep in mind that the shell holes were very big and the mud around them as slippery as ice. Even a man who fell into a hole often could not get a hold to climb out. In addition to these horrific conditions, both man and beast would often be trapped in the shell hole while under heavy gunfire and bombing.

Most, if not all, of the ammunition was transported to the big guns by horse, mule, and wagon. The Germans made every effort to stop them by any means possible.

One battle was at Vimy Ridge, which the Allies would not have taken if it hadn't been for the horses and mules that kept a steady supply of ammunition coming to the fighting men. After the ridge was taken, it was the cavalry on horseback that chased the Germans and cleaned up the towns and villages along the way.

In Italy, most of the horses were Percherons that were shipped from the United States. Six of these heavy draft horses were needed to haul one heavy, 149-millimeter gun.

THE "OLD BLACKS"—GUN HORSES

One of the most famous teams of gun horses was "The Old Blacks." This team was assigned to the F Battery, Royal Horse Artillery. This team was unique in that it stayed together throughout the war and all of the horses survived. Their jobs and the battles in which they worked were no less severe than any other team of horses, but the drivers of this team were especially diligent in caring for them.

After the war, the horses were used for a number of parades and had the honor of pulling the gun carriage of the Unknown Warrior to Westminster Abbey. All of the horses were eventually retired and placed in good homes, where they received excellent care for the rest of their lives.

The Old Blacks.

CAVALRY

When many people think of the cavalry, the image of men in blue uniforms riding in a column in the Old West comes to mind. The Old West cavalry has been romanticized by Hollywood movies; however, mounted troops are as old as the first time men rode horses to fight in wars.

With the advent of tanks and other vehicles of war in World War I, the role of the cavalry was not considered as important as it had been previously. What history does show us is that the cavalry did make a difference in the Great War. The cavalry is so entrenched in military history that units still bear the name "Cavalry." These modern cavalry divisions are typically a part of the armor and aviation units of the army.

Historical records show that it was the British cavalry units in World War I that played a significant part in winning battles in Palestine and Syria. It was also noted that both General Hunter Liggett and General von Kluck felt that, if they had a stronger cavalry unit, they could have captured the retreating Axis forces.

During the initial fighting near Mons (Belgium), the Germans attacked the British so severely that they were forced to retreat. However, an attack by the 2nd Cavalry Brigade, both mounted and dismounted, to the German flanks, gave the British three hours to organize their retreat and saved lives. An official report by Field Marshal Lord Haig stated, "Throughout the great retirement in 1914, our cavalry covered the retirement and protected the flanks of our columns against the onrush of the enemy, and on frequent occasions prevented our infantry from being over-run by the enemy cavalry" (Baynes, *Animal Heroes of the Great War*, 37).

A remarkable cavalry charge reminiscent of the cavalry glory days occurred in October 1917. Under the direction of General Allenby (a devoted cavalry-man), two regiments of Australian cavalry made a night march in unknown territory at Gaza to position themselves for an attack on the Turks.

It was around dusk, and the enemy trenches were outlined by Turkish rifle fire and British bombs bursting overhead. The cavalry, half hidden in dust, charged the trenches. The sound of the shells bursting drowned out the sound of their hooves. The horses leaped over two enemy trenches and then the Australian soldiers dismounted and fought hand-to-hand with their bayonets. Within ten minutes they had captured 2,000 Turks and killed 500; only 64 Aussies were dead or wounded.

The Gaza area of Egypt where the war was being waged was a desert. Like any area that has little or no water, the war became a war for water. As the Turks retreated, they destroyed the wells so that the Allies would not have access to water. Despite the hardships, the horses of Allenby's cavalry continued on, sometimes going seventy hours without water. They were often so exhausted after a day of battle that they refused to eat. The soldiers, being completely devoted to their mounts, would take the dry grains, knead them with a few drops of water into small balls, and feed their horse by hand so that the horses would survive.

On longer marches, cavalrymen would keep small amounts of water in tins on the dashboards of guns and wagons, and every hour they would stop, dampen a small cloth, and wipe the horses' eyes, nostrils, and mouths. The horses were taken care of before a soldier tended to his own needs, and this sustained the horses until water was available for them to drink. The soldiers were so devoted to their horses that they never considered quenching their own thirst with the water for the horses.

The Turks were successful in stalling the British pursuit and were able to stand up to the British. A very small cavalry division—less than a squadron—charged the Turks, who shot them point blank as they charged. Despite the odds, few Turks survived yet 95 of the 175 cavalrymen were unhurt. This charge was impressive, because it was the first time that the cavalrymen used the then-modern thrusting sword. (A thrusting sword was slightly curved and stiffer than the older swords.) This victory was important because the British captured an important Turkish codebook and heavy artillery.

Another famous cavalry charge occurred near Jerusalem at El Mughar. The Turks were positioned on a high ridge that was inaccessible to ground troops. The cavalry again took to the field under attack from artillery and rifle fire. They had to travel two miles to the objective over open ground. The mounts climbed up the sides of a steep water course, got onto the plain, and trotted until they were a half mile from the objective. There they advanced at a fast canter. When they were 100 yards from the objective, they charged at a full gallop. The Turks were defeated; the British captured 1,500 prisoners and killed 600 of the enemy. The cavalry lost only 129 officers and men, and 265 horses were killed or wounded.

The cavalry went on to pursue the remaining Turks for up to 200 miles. As the Turks surrendered, the cavalry would round them up and contain them. After the Turks had been captured, the cavalry was ordered to patrol the area in order to prevent looting by the locals.

After the areas west of the Jordan were secured, the cavalry moved toward Damascus. The cavalry was not able to replace the horses that were too exhausted to work or the ones that had been killed in battle. Because of the shortage of horses, only guns, ammunition wagons, and light ambulances were brought with the units. The men carried two days' worth of rations, and when those were finished, they had to live off of the land. They were able to do this for an entire year.

The final victory of the World War I cavalry was in October 2, 1918, when the 3rd Australian Light Horse Brigade galloped more than six miles under fire and attacked the Turks with their swords. The cavalry was responsible for the destruction of three Turkish armies and the capture of more than 25,000 prisoners.

During World War I, George S. Patton was a major (later to become a general) who specialized in tank warfare. But he was a great lover of and believer in horses. He is quoted as saying, "The horse exists in large numbers. His pattern is 'sealed' by the Creator and is not subject to constant and expensive alterations. He is not produced by the sinful rich, nor bred by corporations; he is the God-given property of the Common people. By maintaining cavalry and horsed artillery we shall continue to benefit the largest and most worthy class of our constituents, the Farmers of America" (Baynes, *Animal Heroes of the Great War,* 48).

Unlike the draft horses, which came primarily from the United States, the cavalry horses were mostly bred in Italy. The Italian cavalry horses had to be trained to negotiate the wet, swampy land, the rivers, and the high cliffs.

In general, cavalry horses showed an amazing ability to adapt to war situations. They learned to recognize the bugle calls and respond accordingly. They showed an amazing amount of courage. In one battle, a shell hit the ground just behind a horse. The horse bolted from the spot, but when the shell did not explode, the horse returned to his station, smelled the shell, and stood as he was taught to do.

It is interesting that the Bible speaks of the attitude of the horse in battle, and the accounts of World War I seem to be exactly as the Old Testament describes. "Its (the horse's)

Wipers riding a horse.

majestic snorting is terrible. It paws violently, exults mightily; it goes out to meet the weapons. It laughs at fear, and is not dismayed; it does not turn back from the sword. Upon it rattle the quiver, the flashing spear, and the javelin. With fierceness and rage it swallows the ground; it cannot stand still at the sound of the trumpet. When the trumpet sounds, it says 'Aha!' From a distance it smells the battle, the thunder of the captains, and the shouting" (Job 39:20-25, NRSV).

One of the most colorful of the cavalry units was the Algerian Spahis, who had a long history of service and were assigned to the French cavalry. With a mix of traditional colorful Arabian uniforms, they were quite a sight mounted on their white Arabian horses.

As with the other animals of war, the soldiers did the best they could to take care of the horses. However, because many of the soldiers had not grown up caring for horses, the army assigned men to each division to teach the soldiers horse-care skills. Many soldiers suffered cold, discomfort, and hunger to take special care of their mounts.

In one instance, a soldier spent the night in the cold rain rubbing his horse's belly. The horse had colic and would fuss if the man did not rub his belly. The soldier had draped his blanket over the horse to keep him warm. Fortunately, a veterinarian nearby in another unit was able to bring the medicine the horse needed.

Although the cavalry was not a main component of the Great War due to the fact that horses were not effective in trench warfare, some generals insisted upon having their charger nearby. Because of the nature of the war, these horses were subjected to the dangers of battle but also found their way into the hearts of the soldiers. According to Major-General J.E.B. Seely, "If you are to be seen by a number of soldiers you must ride a horse. If you go on your feet you are lost in the crowd; if you go in a motor car, you either block the traffic on the road to which you are confined, or pass so swiftly that no one knows you are there" (Baker, *Animal War Heroes,* 74).

WARRIOR THE BAY THOROUGHBRED

Warrior was the charger for Major-General Seely and was raised on Seely's farm in the Isle of Wight. His mother was a black, Irish-bred Thoroughbred known for her even temperament. When the war broke out, Seely took Warrior with him to France, and if Seely was not riding Warrior in battle, Sir John French or other officers rode the horse.

Warrior, it seemed, led a charmed life, which did not go unnoticed by the troops. Other men and horses were often shot and killed next to Warrior, but he remained unhurt.

Warrior was a very intelligent horse and learned to tell the difference between shell fire and rifle fire. He learned that conditions were safer under shell fire and would remain calm, yet machine-gun or rifle fire made him nervous. Seely noticed that, if Warrior was in the midst of shell fire, he would continue his charge without worry, but if he heard the ping of bullets, he would, on his own, swerve to avoid the stream of bullets.

On one occasion, Warrior was standing side-by-side with another horse when a shell exploded next to them. A groom was holding both horses and recounted that the horse next to Warrior was literally cut in two, but Warrior, covered in blood, was unhurt and perfectly calm. On another occasion, just as Warrior was taken out of a stable on a farm, a shell hit the stable right behind him. Again, Warrior remained calm.

Seely had two other horses and would sometimes ride them instead of Warrior. But Warrior was as devoted to Seely as a pet dog and would follow Seely without a saddle or bridle. The first time he did this, Warrior literally jumped out of his stall to follow his human companion.

On another occasion, Warrior was stabled in a room in a house. It was rather unusual because the room still had furniture in it and hardwood floors. Seely was instructing his troops nearby when he heard an explosion. He ran to Warrior, fearing the worst. He found Warrior with his head stuck out of a window. A beam was lying across his back, and before Seely could help him, Warrior leaped out of the window, just as the rest of the house collapsed around him.

Sabotage or a horrible accident almost killed Warrior on another occasion. Someone either purposely or accidentally put hundreds of metal hooks into the feed hay for the horses. Many horses died from eating them, because the hooks lodged in their stomachs and intestines. Warrior did swallow one of the hooks, but instead of suffering quietly like the other horses, he became violent. He rolled, leaped, and kicked so hard that no one could get near him. As luck would have it, he was able to dislodge the hook and he passed it without further trouble, although he did take a few weeks to recover.

Warrior survived many fierce battles in which other horses were killed. He was never wounded even though he became a target of the German army. After the war, he returned home with Seely to live a peaceful life.

RAGTIME THE ARABIAN

Ragtime, or Raggie as he was called, was born in India in 1910. He was the personal horse for Lord Middleton. Raggie was a well-bred horse; his mother was Gladrags and his sire Geneva, an Arabian. Raggie took after his Arabian father in looks and size.

On the way to the front to rejoin Middleton, Raggie was almost stolen by an Arab. It seems that bands of Arabs would snipe at the camp of soldiers and steal everything they could. One Arab in particular tried to steal Raggie, but he was caught by a sentry.

Just like the other animals who served in the Middle East, Raggie had to endure long marches in terrible heat, often without food or water. Raggie and his two stablemates, Galopia and Alphonse, were cared for as best as circumstances permitted.

Ragtime.

During troop movements, the three horses had to be transported by a small boat that did not have a gangplank for the horses to unload. In order to get the horses on shore, they had to jump over the side of the boat to the bank about ten feet below.

Alphonse, who was the most experienced jumper, went first and landed on his chest and head. Next came Raggie, who landed similarly next to Alphonse. Lastly and calmly came Galopia, who landed on the backs of the other two horses. None were hurt, but all were rather annoyed and stood stamping and snorting their displeasure.

In the summer of 1916, Lord Middleton and his horses were separated. Middleton had to return to India and the horses were sent to one of the remount stations. Raggie was sent to a cavalry regiment; ironically, it was the one to which he had originally been assigned. He recognized some of the men and horses that were still in the regiment.

When the war was over, Raggie was used as a polo pony. It was at one of these matches that Middleton saw Raggie again and was able to purchase him.

However, Raggie's military career was not over. Middleton was serving with the 10th Lancers in 1918 when an Arab rebellion broke out and Middleton rode Raggie. Many of the horses that served in this military action died from exhaustion. But Raggie's stamina and Arabian blood kept him alive.

Raggie went on to serve as Middleton's mount in the Governor's Bodyguard as a trumpeter's mount. He often escorted the state carriage at important functions. After a brief separation in 1923 when Middleton returned to England, Raggie was reunited with Middleton and spent the rest of his life with him. Raggie was awarded five medals for his service in the war—three for the Great War service, one for the Arab rebellion, and one for long service and good conduct.

CHARLIE THE HUNTER

Charlie belonged to Colonel E.J. Harrison, who was assigned to the 6th Rifle Battalion (the King's Liverpool Regiment). Charlie served throughout the war, from 1915 to 1919, and survived many battles.

Charlie was another horse who handled the shells and the gunfire of war in a very calm manner. He was never wounded but was sent to "sick bay" twice. Once he caught a cold and contracted pneumonia, and a few years later he became so thin and weak from serving at the front that he had to be sent to the hospital to recover.

For some reason that no one could fathom, Charlie did not like the sight of the draft dogs that pulled the equipment. He would become quite unmanageable and would rear and try to bolt. Eventually he tolerated the dogs, but he never liked them and did his best to avoid them. Harrison could not understand Charlie's behavior, because the horse had grown up around dogs and had not minded them at that time. However, Harrison figured out the problem when he noticed that Charlie did not mind the carting dogs when they were not in a cart. Apparently, Charlie was upset with the carts, or with the dogs when they were in harness.

After the war, Charlie was included in reviews and parades. He was always right behind the band, and because he was a favorite of the soldiers, the drummer would hold a piece of sugar in his hand behind his back as a treat for Charlie. Of course, Charlie enjoyed this very much and would toss his head and snort with pleasure. He also had a trick that he liked to do, and, when he was able, he would hit the drum with his nose and bridle, making a big bang.

Harrison was wounded in the war and sent home earlier than Charlie. But it wasn't long before Charlie was shipped home to Harrison, and he arrived at the train station a few miles from Harrison's farm. When Harrison rode Charlie toward home, Charlie seemed to remember where he was. Just to test this, Harrison tried to ride him past the gates to the farm, but Charlie refused to go and headed straight for the gates.

An unexplained incident happened on Charlie's homecoming, as told by Baker in *Animal War Heroes*. Charlie had a stablemate from his pre-war days—a small, old pony that was normally quiet and docile. Charlie's old stablemate rarely neighed or carried on. Yet two hours before Charlie returned home, the old pony started neighing, as if calling out to Charlie, and he restlessly trotted around the paddock. "This may seem almost incredible, but the simple fact remains that the little pony behaved in a most peculiar manner for two hours previous to Charlie's return, and stood leaning over the hedge close to the gates waiting to welcome him. He could not possibly have seen Charlie coming, since there were two hedges, a tennis court, and some gardens completely screening the paddock from the road" (Baker, 92).

The two old friends made a big fuss over each other for quite awhile.

After the war ended, horsemanship schools were started to give the soldiers something to do while they waited the months it could take to be shipped home. The soldiers learned how to compete in horse shows; in pulling competitions, jumping, polo, and equitation, which is a working competition that includes dressage (horses move to music); and in ease of handling, such as overcoming obstacles that they would encounter in a field within a certain period of time. The riding style might also demonstrate the styles used in different countries.

CHAPTER 7

CAMELS

TRANSPORT CAMELS

Camels also played a significant role in World War I as transport animals. Imagine the sight they made, marching two by two, led by an Egyptian camel driver dressed in a blue, flowing robe.

The most important cargo that the camels carried was drinking water for the soldiers. General Allenby used about 40,000 camels to support his troops in their attack against the Turks. The military initially hired camel drivers and their camels to transport water for the soldiers, but it quickly became obvious that the civilians did not want to participate in actual battle. General Allenby therefore formed the Camel Transport Group in Egypt. The camels were government owned and the drivers were enlisted men.

This goal took a huge effort to accomplish. The army first tried to use Indian camels, but they were plains animals and not suited for the desert. Most of them died because they would lick the sand, which caused sand colic and stomach ulcerations. Next the army tried to procure camels from the western desert region, but this did not succeed because of hostility from local tribes.

The last attempt was successful, because the army went through the proper political channels in the Algiers, Somaliland, and delta regions of North Africa. They put the burden of obtaining camels on the local sheiks. The army would tell them how many camels they needed, and the sheiks acquired them from their tribes.

When the camels arrived they were checked by army veterinarians. If they passed inspection, they were shipped by boat and then by rail to Egypt.

The camels were not easy to handle and would panic and stampede at unusual sights, sounds, or smells. Some went "mad" and had to be destroyed. Some, in their panic, would try to attack soldiers. A camel could easily grab a man by the leg or arm and fling him through the air.

The Camel Transport Corps included about 20 companies which consisted of about 2,000 camels each. The rest were kept at remount depots where sick, wounded, or worn-out animals were replaced. Toward the end of the war the army had to enlist female or cow camels, which, although they were more docile than the males, posed a new problem—their giving birth on the marches. The baby camels could not keep up with the column and so the soldiers devised a "camel net." Babies were placed in the nets and then put on the backs of the mothers. Every six hours or so, they would stop to let the babies nurse.

The army eventually learned that camels were not hardy animals and instead were rather delicate. Many of the animals died from exposure due to heat, rain, and cold. They also suffered from many diseases, and most of the camels had one or more. The only reason the Camel Corps succeeded was because replacements were available. For example, General Skobeleff lost all but one of his 12,000 camels when he campaigned in Central Asia. Because of the high occurrence of disease in camels, the army formed special veterinary-staffed camel hospitals.

The other major problem the army encountered was obtaining enough light, highly adjustable saddles for the camels. When a camel started a campaign, it would have a large hump and a layer of fat. As it went without water and food, it would end up a lot smaller than when it started out. As a result, the saddle had to be adjusted as the camel became smaller. If the saddle did not fit properly, it would cause sores. The camels also needed blankets and halters.

It was also challenging for the troops to figure out how frequently they should water the camels because there was no set rule. The amount of water a camel needed depended on the nature of the campaign and the environment in which it worked. Furthermore, the camels could not be watered at a lake or river because if they got their feet wet they would develop foot problems. The soldiers ended up designing watering troughs for the camels to solve this problem. And, although a camel could drink up to twenty-five gallons of water at a time, it usually drank this amount in two sessions. Because some camels drank more slowly they would end up leaving with their companions whether or not they had drunk enough water.

The main source of fresh water came from the Sweet Water Canal, which was located on the western side of the Suez Canal. This, in turn, was fed by the Nile River. The water was filtered at a plant and then loaded into tanker trucks and driven to railheads. Next it was put into canvas cisterns, where it was then put into the metal tanks that were carried by the camels.

The camel's foot was designed to walk on sand—the foot would spread out and cushion the camel. But when the cold rains hit the units, the camel's foot had nothing with which to grip the slick mud, which was like ice. Some camels would fall down and others were able to get up again, but many of them fell to their death. To their credit, the animals worked with all the heart they could muster.

In one instance fifty camels were traveling when a shell burst near them, killing about half of them. When an officer went to the area where the camels had been, he saw local Arabs cutting up the dead animals and hauling away the meat. The wounded camels were calm and quietly chewing cud rather than acting upset (Baynes, *Animal Heroes of the Great War*, 86).

The camels were fed in either troughs or in feed cloths to prevent them from eating sand. When the area was suitable the camels were allowed to graze, but problems occurred with that as well. The grazing area had to be searched for poisonous plants because if the plant was not local for the camel the animal would not recognize it and would eat it. Just a mouthful of oleander with grass would kill most camels.

Snakes were also a threat, and a poisonous snakebite would often kill a camel, despite its large size. Fortunately if a camel was bitten by a snake, it would bellow until it went into a coma. This saved many from death because a veterinarian or camel driver could take care of the animal immediately and often save its life.

All camels had to be groomed daily, which they seemed to enjoy. A grooming session took about half an hour because the caretaker had to make sure that all ticks were removed. If the camels were near a large, deep body of water, they were allowed to bathe and swim, which they also appreciated.

The camels were not easy to live with or care for. Most of the military camels were males, which were noted for their bad, unpredictable temperaments. The camels were not affectionate toward their handlers.

One advantage in using camels was that they would lie quietly near gunfire. However, they often did panic at the slightest sound. If they panicked they often broke their picket ropes and would stampede through a camp, barging into tents and harming anyone who got in their way.

Camels would tolerate their keepers but no one else. During the mating season, which usually lasted from December to March, the males might refuse to eat and drink their normal amount of food and water. During this time, camels could "go mad" or be "in must." When this happened, they would charge, and a

A "mad" camel.

large pick bladder that is part of the soft palate would hang from their mouths. Although they typically would not harm their caretakers, they were known to kill anyone else who came near them. Some of the "mad" camels had to be tied and muzzled, and some might bite off a leg or arm of anyone who got within their range. "Mad" camels were known to have grabbed a man by the leg or arm and run off, swinging them in the air. Some would lie down on a man or kneel on him and crush him to death. Humans were not the only victims of "mad" camels; they would often attack other camels and do considerable damage.

Even though the camels were often dangerous and hard to handle, they were worth the trouble and risk because a large one could carry up to 350 pounds with ease. In certain conditions, they were often forced to carry double that weight. In good conditions, they could travel three miles in an hour.

Camels were also used to transport wounded soldiers using one of two devices for this purpose. For soldiers who could sit up, a chair-like device would

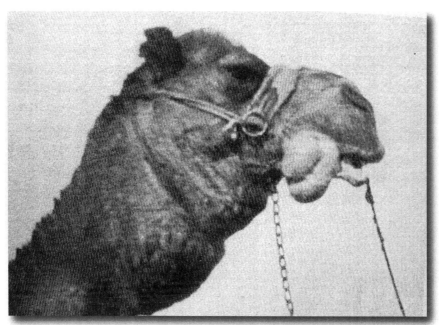

A "mad" camel "in must."

hang on either side of the camel, allowing the camel to carry two men at a time. If they could not sit up, a cradle-like device with an awning permitted the men to lie prone and be protected from the sun.

However, riding on a camel was not a pleasant experience. Camels have three basic gaits; bad, badder, and baddest. A short walk is like rolling on a rough ocean in a small boat, a long walk intensifies the short walk, a trot is even worse, and a gallop is a bone-jarring experience. Yet this tortuous method of transportation was better than dying a slow death in the sun or freezing rain.

SWIFT CAMELS

A number of units employed camels in the same manner as cavalry horses. Some of these units were the Bikaner Camel Corps, the Arab Camel Corps, the Egyptian Camel Corps, and the Imperial Camel Corps.

The soldiers would ride the camels into battle, where they would dismount and fight as infantry. These animals could travel swiftly and still carry a total of about 400 pounds each, which included the rider and supplies.

Swift camels had two seated saddles, one for the rider and the other for supplies. However, in certain cases, two men would ride one camel.

Many people know the story of Lawrence of Arabia. It was after the capture of Amman that Colonel T.E. Lawrence led the Sharifian troops and the Arab Camel Corps against the Turks. As depicted in the movies, Colonel Lawrence would lead his troops, either on horseback or on a camel, on a wild charge across the desert to capture a train with the goal of interrupting railroad communications.

The Germans would send planes to bomb the troops, but Lawrence would have his troops hide in a wadi (a valley or dry riverbed), with the camels lying down behind the black rocks, hidden from the Germans. They would hide for several days and nights and then attack a passing train.

Although the camels did not endear themselves to the soldiers the way other animals did, they made transportation possible where no other animal could have succeeded. They died and worked as hard as any and were responsible for making campaigns successful.

CHAPTER 8

DONKEYS AND OXEN

DONKEYS

Many of us do not think of donkeys as serving in wartime. However, they did, and they were loyal and patient and could carry an amazing amount of weight for their size. The most common donkey was the Poitou donkey of France, a very gentle, steady breed. The Poitou has an unusual coat, which is long and soft and, when not brushed, hangs in long cords.

The Poitous are almost always dark brown or black, with a white underbelly and white rings around the eyes and nose. They are also very large—fourteen to fifteen hands in height (a hand is about four inches)—which is about the size of an average Arabian horse. They have very long ears that mostly flop over rather than stand upright. Unfortunately, very few Poitous remain in the world today.

What made these donkeys so versatile in the field is that they would work until they dropped. They could carry up to 200 pounds of weight or pull and push equipment.

The soldiers who were either too old or too infirm to fight in the trenches were assigned to handle the donkeys. Because of their smaller size, the donkeys could be led right into the trenches to distribute food and supplies, but that meant that they had to work at night.

The Italians used donkeys for mountain transport because they were surefooted. The donkeys were groomed every morning, fed well, and kept in barracks that were heated by little stoves. Records show that few of the donkeys had to be vetted and then mostly from rope abrasions.

Donkeys are curious animals, and one Italian officer told of an incident where a train of donkeys carrying ammunition in the Alps encountered an artillery bombardment. All of the donkeys, with their ears cocked forward, went to the edge of the trail, and, looking toward the enemy, they started to bray loudly. The Italians were very amused and joined in, waving their hats in the air (Baynes, *Animal Heroes of the Great War*, 128-129).

Other breeds of donkeys were used in the Middle East. They ranged in size and color; the large white Hassawi donkeys were especially valued. The donkeys were so hardy that they could work for twenty-four hours without food or water. On one occasion a pack of about 200 donkeys had to travel forty miles round-trip to deliver ammunition to an area where there was heavy fighting over rough terrain and the risk of being attacked at any time. They were very successful in their mission.

OXEN

There is scant information about the oxen that served in World War I, but serve they did. Because they are slow, very strong and steady, they were used to pull the heaviest equipment. Unfortunately, because of their size they were easy targets. Because they were often used in teams when they were subjected to attacks, more than one was killed at the same time.

Unlike the camels, when oxen saw dead oxen, they seemed to become fearful and would be reluctant to work. Once a pair of oxen were teamed together, they liked to work only with their team mate.

According to Baynes, the oxen suffered the most during the war, especially in the African campaign. They were subject to disease, especially from ticks and the tsetse fly. In the African campaign alone, over sixty thousand oxen were used and most of them died from diseases (Baynes, *Animal Heroes of the Great War*, 143-145).

Donkeys and oxen have been used throughout the world since the beginning of history. For the most part they are gentle animals that have remarkable abilities to carry weight, and endure hardships. When Americans were settling the old west oxen were often used by pioneers instead of horses on wagon trains. This is because even though the oxen were slower than the horse, the oxen were more likely to survive the harsh conditions when horses could not.

Many prospectors had a donkey as a companion because of their surefootedness and ability to carry supplies. Both donkeys and oxen earned the respect and love of the soldier in World War I.

CHAPTER 9

VETERINARY CORPS

In view of the fact that animals have been involved in all wars in one form or another, it is a bit surprising that the American army did not establish an independent Veterinary Corps until 1916. Prior to 1916, the veterinarians who were in the military were part of the Quartermaster Corps.

Wounded dog being cared for.

When the Veterinary Corps was formed, there was a severe shortage of trained veterinarians to enlist. After all efforts were made, only sixty-two veterinarians were available to care for tens of thousands of war animals. Realizing that they needed help forming the new corps, the American army called upon the British, who had a well-established Veterinary Corps.

Under the guidance of Colonel J.J. Aitken of the British Veterinary Corps, the Americans had the Veterinary Corps of the National Army established by October 4, 1917. By contacting all possible sources, the Veterinary Corps was able to grow to 2,313 veterinary officers for the duration of the war. Often, men who were unfit for overseas duty were used as aides or veterinary technicians.

The job of the American Veterinary Corps was to prepare, heal, and examine the animals that were to be shipped overseas. This was a near-impossible task because the hospitals were inadequate and illness was a big problem. Because there was only about one soldier per fifteen animals, they could not be cared for properly.

Things were not much better in France or Italy, where they had to transport fresh animals (mainly horses) to the soldiers and transport the sick and injured to the hospitals for treatment. Horses were essential for the mobility of the army, and there were never enough fresh, healthy, strong horses to meet the need.

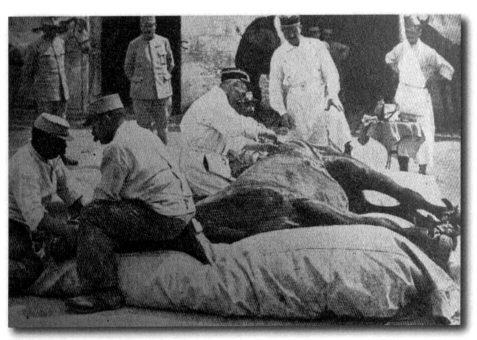

Horse in surgery.

The British Army Veterinary Corps set an example for the rest of the world by keeping their armies supplied with horses and mules. The main reason why the British were so successful is the fact that their corps was established long before the war started. The British had learned how important animals were to a war effort in the 1899–1902 conflict with South Africa. They learned valuable lessons from this war and established a stellar corps as a result.

Of all of the wounded and sick horses and mules sent to the hospitals, fully 85 percent were able to return to service, were cured, and/or were healed. The tax-

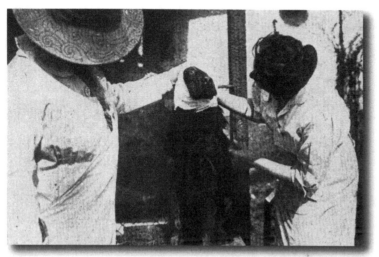

War dog getting his head bandaged.

payers' money funded the Veterinary Corps, and they found out that it was much less expensive to heal a wounded animal than it was to buy and possibly have to train a new one.

Because of the logistics of shipping large animals back to America and England, many of them were left behind. But on a happy note, just as the Allied forces adopted animals captured during the war, so did the Germans. In an article that first appeared in the *American Legion Monthly* (November 1936, page 40), a picture shows a German man with a captured American horse. The article goes on to explain that the Germans valued the animals and gave them love and exceptional care. And so, there was a happy ending for some of the gallant steeds that served in World War I.

Horse being treated for skin disorders.

SOURCES CONSULTED

ARTICLES

La Vie Militaire, "L'Armée et le Chien de Trait", June 5, 1912 (no author listed).

Our Dogs, "A Canine Camp in France", December 10, 1915 (no author listed).

The Illustrated War News, "Dogs of War on its Merciful Side: A French Red Cross Section, with Canine Helpers, Leaving for the Front," February 17, 1915 (no author).

Le Miroir, "Les Chiens Du Front," May 27, 1917 (no author).

Illingworth, Frank, "Dogs Have Always Helped in Wars," *The American Kennel Gazette,* January 1, 1940.

Jedda, Barbara, "Fearless Soldiers, Faithful Friends," *AKC Gazette,* April 1996.

BOOKS

Baker, Peter Shaw. *Animal War Heroes.* London: A. &.C. Black, Ltd., 1933.

Baynes, Ernest Harold. *Animal Heroes of the Great War.* New York: The MacMillan Co., 1925.

Bulanda, Susan. *God's Creatures: A Biblical View of Animals.* Greeley, CO: Cladach Publishing, 2008.

Richardson, E.H. Lieutenant-Colonel. *Watch Dogs: Their Training and Management.* London: Hutchinson & Co., 1924.

Richardson, E.H. Lieutenant-Colonel. *Forty Years with Dogs.* Philadelphia: David McKay Co., 1928.

Richardson, E.H. Lieutenant-Colonel, and Richardson, Mrs. Blanche. *Fifty Years With Dogs*. London: Hutchinson & Co., n.d. (post 1938).

Richardson, E.H. Lieutenant-Colonel. *War, Police and Watch Dogs*. London: William Blackwood and Sons, 1910.

WEBSITES
HYPERLINK "http://www.governorsfootguard.com/stubby/"

ABOUT THE AUTHOR

Recognized as a dog trainer since 1963, Susan Bulanda has worked with dogs in a variety of fields. She is recognized worldwide as an expert in canine search and rescue (SAR) and as a canine and feline behavior consultant.

She is certified with the International Association of Animal Behavior Consultants and has served both as its vice president and dog chairperson.

As an adjunct professor at Kutztown University, Susan developed two programs for the Career Development Center: Canine Training and Management Program: Levels I and II–for students who want to become dog trainers and canine behavior consultants.

She has won numerous awards, including the prestigious Maxwell Award from the Dog Writers Association of America, has lectured worldwide, and has written hundreds of articles.

Her books include:
READY! Training the Search and Rescue Dog
Ready to Serve, Ready to Save: Strategies of Real-Life Search and Rescue Missions
Scenting on the Wind: Scentwork for Hunting Dogs
Boston Terriers
Faithful Friends: Holocaust Survivors' Stories of the Pets Who Gave Them Comfort, Suffered Alongside Them, and Waited for Their Return
God's Creatures: A Biblical View of Animals

To view them, browse her website at www.sbulanda.com.